The Gurkha Diaries of
Robert Atkins MC

Robert Everett William Atkins
b.20/1/1927

The Gurkha Diaries of Robert Atkins MC

Robert Atkins

Historical Commentaries by
Brigadier C.J. Bullock OBE, MC

Pen & Sword
MILITARY

First published in Great Britain in 2021 by
Pen & Sword Military
An imprint of
Pen & Sword Books Ltd
Yorkshire – Philadelphia

ISBN 978 1 39909 145 9

Typeset by Mac Style
Printed and bound in the UK by CPI Group (UK) Ltd,
Croydon, CR0 4YY.

Pen & Sword Books Limited incorporates the imprints of Atlas,
Archaeology, Aviation, Discovery, Family History, Fiction, History,
Maritime, Military, Military Classics, Politics, Select, Transport,
True Crime, Air World, Frontline Publishing, Leo Cooper, Remember
When, Seaforth Publishing, The Praetorian Press, Wharncliffe
Local History, Wharncliffe Transport, Wharncliffe True Crime
and White Owl.

For a complete list of Pen & Sword titles please contact

PEN & SWORD BOOKS LIMITED
47 Church Street, Barnsley, South Yorkshire, S70 2AS, England
E-mail: enquiries@pen-and-sword.co.uk
Website: www.pen-and-sword.co.uk

Or

PEN AND SWORD BOOKS
1950 Lawrence Rd, Havertown, PA 19083, USA
E-mail: Uspen-and-sword@casematepublishers.com
Website: www.penandswordbooks.com

For my Anabel

Contents

Acknowledgements

I would firstly like to thank David and Catherine Barham, who read my father's diaries and then gave them to their good friend Peter Duffell, who they thought would enjoy reading them. Peter then passed them on to Henry Wilson at Pen & Sword, who said that they were definitely worth publishing. This was very exciting news to us all, and I am so grateful to Henry and all of his team at Pen & Sword, who have been a complete delight to work with.

A huge thank you to Peter Duffell for so generously writing the foreword and to Christopher Bullock for his excellent introductory commentaries, which set the scene for my father's service in India and Malaya; and to George Chamier for editing the book on behalf of Pen & Sword.

The 6th Gurkha Rifles Regimental Association and particularly John Anderson and Brian O'Bree together with Dr Daren Bowyer and Doug Henderson of the Gurkha Museum were hugely helpful not least in sourcing many of the photographs that illustrate the book.

Just prior to the news of the diaries being published, we had decided to have the handwritten manuscript typed out, a long task which was kindly taken on by my cousin's son Daniel Downden after his GCSEs. Our thanks go to him and to Caroline Lewis, Simon Jessel and Theo Jessel, who were all instrumental in getting this done.

My father suffered a stroke only three months after completing his manuscript, which by the way he wrote without consulting an actual diary; it was all handwritten from memory.

My parents are now into their 65th year of marriage. They are without doubt the two most influential people in my life and the most loving parents and grandparents. Our family have so much to thank them for.

We are all so proud of what Robert has achieved, and what better way to tell the next generation about his adventures in India and Malaya than in this beautiful book.

Vicky Greenley
London, 2021

Foreword

Lieutenant General Sir Peter Duffell KCB, CBE, MC

As I write in early 2021, Robert Atkins is ninety-four and living with his wife, Anabel, in the quintessentially English village of Rolvenden Layne on the Kent/Sussex border. Almost ten years previously, in December 2011, Robert, always a fit and healthy man as befits a one-time Army boxing champion, suffered a carotid arterial stroke that affected his speech and ability to write; a plight that he has borne with the greatest stoicism.

Fortuitously, just prior to this wretched ill-fortune, and largely for the benefit of his grandchildren, Robert set down in a firm, well-rounded and legible hand a detailed account of his early life – one markedly different from that which he was later to enjoy after his soldiering was over. These diaries tell of a young Army officer's journey of singular travel and excitement. As the Second World War drew to a close, Robert had set out for India, where his father and grandfather had served before him, armed with a commission in the Indian Army. At the modest age of eighteen he was to join the elite 8th Gurkha Rifles. Then, following Partition and the Independence of India in 1947, he transferred to the British Army along with four of the ten Gurkha Regiments of the Indian Army. Three years later, Robert returned to the East and his former soldiers, and for seven years he was to serve with the First Battalion of the 6th Gurkha Rifles in Malaya. Finally, in 1958 Robert together with his Regiment moved to Hong Kong, and while still a relatively young man, in the uncertainties of the time, he resigned his commission, left the East and with his young family sought new challenges in England.

By chance my wife, Ann, had been brought up in the village of Rolvenden, just next door to the home of Robert and Anabel Atkins. In 2019, during a visit that we paid to Ann's old home, a mutual village friend, David Barham, told me for the first time about Robert's diaries; how they had captivated him and that I, as a former Gurkha officer, should certainly read them. David generously agreed to send me a photocopy of the handwritten portfolio, and two volumes of diaries soon arrived with me.

The diaries were not written for publication so they include some family events and non-operational detail; but they have not been edited in any way and, as such, they give a rounded picture of the author's military life. Robert writes of imperial times that are now long gone and an age that has now almost vanished. His vivid recollections – no more than fragments of history – were set down on paper some fifty years or more after they occurred. The diaries are beautifully written with much literary merit and value; catching with a young man's observant eye the individual character, hazards and flavour of historic events in India and Malaya. And Robert captures them with a freshness and immediacy that almost suggests they were written the day after they occurred. In that respect Robert deservedly entitles them 'diaries'. If one wants to know and feel what it was like to grapple with the horrors on the railways and roads of India during Partition or to seek out ruthless terrorists based deep in the Malayan jungle, then one should read these diaries.

The first volume – *An Indian Diary* – covers life as a fresh, newly commissioned subaltern in the 8th Gurkha Rifles. The war is almost over, and Robert's account embraces the ending of the Raj and the British presence in India, an inevitable and belated grant of Independence and all the agonies of Partition with its horrendous violence as India is divided along sectarian lines.

Robert Atkins is just twenty, and his carefree lifestyle as a young, adventurous subaltern is suddenly swept aside by events as he bears witness to scenes of unimaginable horror: Hindu, Sikh and Muslim attack each other with untold ferocity, while Robert and his impartial Gurkhas battle to provide a measure of succour and safety to the thousands of refugees fleeing north and south throughout Bengal and the Punjab in desperate attempts to escape the killing fields and find sanctuary. Robert brings the same clarity of unsentimental writing, observation and verisimilitude to *An Indian Diary* as he does to the later account of his Malayan adventures. An historical record of the raw horror perpetrated by Indians on their fellow countrymen, it is also a remarkable testimony to the contribution that Robert and his Gurkhas make as they attempt to mitigate the massacres and stem the violence in the last days of a teetering Raj.

By chance and before I began to study Robert's second volume covering his adventures in Malaya, another document came into my hands, culled from the National Archives at Kew. It was labelled 'Top Secret' and was dated 27 May 1953. It had been written in Malaya by Lieutenant Colonel Walter Walker, Commanding Officer of Robert's Battalion, and penned during the ten-year long Malayan Emergency. It was a citation recommending the award of the Military Cross for gallantry to one of his officers, Captain Robert Everett William Atkins. The recommendation was endorsed by the Commander-in- Chief.

The document's security classification was justified by the sensitive details it contained – names and places that, if divulged, might have seriously compromised intelligence sources. The citation recounts in stirring detail a dangerous operation carried out in deep Malayan jungle by Robert and his Gurkhas against determined Chinese Communist terrorists. It had resulted in the successful elimination of 'the most arrogant, ruthless and important Communist political and military leader operating in Upper Perak' together with his bodyguards and cohorts. His death was to deal a significant blow to the Communist terrorist organization throughout Malaya.

Robert recalls this operation and many others, without emotion or hyperbole but in gripping detail, through the pages of what he entitled *A Malayan Diary*, an enthralling account of his dangerous campaigning. Like the first diary covering his service in India, Robert transcribed his story from memory, entirely without notes and without corrections or alterations, on one hundred or so closely ruled pages enclosed in a large leather-bound album; a memoir that covers seven years of relentless jungle operations. These took place primarily in Perak, a Malay state that was recognized as a most testing jungle arena in which to seek, find and eliminate the terrorists during a national insurrection that almost brought Malaya to its knees. Robert's seven years of campaigning were interrupted only by some leave in England and a short tour of duty as ADC to the Commander-in-Chief based in Singapore – an occasion that brought a brief respite from jungle operations and, not least, allowed him to win his Anabel!

In all the many regimental records and other published material that cover the ten-year military campaign that was the Malayan Emergency, I have seldom read such a gripping personal account or one that recalls with such refreshing clarity, modesty and sensitive observation the stressful jungle environment in which young Robert Atkins and his formidable Gurkha soldiers operated. It was their robustness, courage and relentless endeavour, along with many others, that eventually delivered peace and prosperity to Malaya in a rare but successful post-war counter-insurgency operation.

Impressed by the compulsive readability and historical value of Robert's diaries, I suggested to my colleague Henry Wilson, commissioning editor of Pen & Sword Books, that his publishing house might like to consider taking on Robert's diaries. Henry was quick to recognize their unique quality, and that they deserved a wider audience and should be published. Christopher Bullock, a distinguished Gurkha Brigadier who had commanded Robert's Regiment with much distinction and had written the definitive work on Gurkha history – *Britain's Gurkhas* – kindly agreed to produce an essential narrative for the diaries to set them in their wider political and military context. He has performed that task with much fluency.

In a break from his campaigning in Malaya Robert married Anabel in Singapore in late 1956. Wedding pictures portray a handsome couple, and they remain people of much character and charm; part of a strong, close family, their contemporary looks belie their age, even if some inevitable physical frailties lie under the surface. The elegant Quince Cottage in Rolvenden Layne has been their home for well over thirty years, and they have lived in the countryside of Kent since Robert left the Army. It was from there that he commuted daily to the City and with great industry and application developed a successful commercial property practice. He remained heavily involved in the industry, working hard, travelling extensively abroad and prospering until he was eighty-three!

Luckily, in spite of his stroke and its wretched impact, Robert remains eminently sharp and alert; there was no paralysis, and he is physically mobile. His cultured enthusiasms for painting in oils and watercolours, for antiques and Persian carpets, for gardening and an extended family, are all intact.

In addition to being a legacy for his family and their wider historical importance, Robert's diaries are a distinguished addition to the burgeoning literary record of Gurkha soldiers. The Gurkhas' detailed story is largely for another place, but these light-hearted and gallant soldiers, recruited from independent Nepal, have loyally served the British Crown for over 200 years. A hundred or more famous battle honours, untold numbers of gallantry decorations and great sacrifice mark their record and have earned them a special and respected place in the van of today's British Army. Robert was proud to belong to that special Gurkha livery; if he has not returned to the scene of the adventures that he records so graphically in his diaries, he certainly remembers his soldiers, their resolution and their charm with the same pride and affection that I do.

I am delighted to introduce Robert Atkins' diaries to a wider audience and I commend them to you.

Part I

An Indian Diary 1944–1947

Introductory Commentary
Brigadier Christopher Bullock

When young Robert Atkins set sail for India in early 1945 to join the 8th Gurkha Rifles little could he have known that he was about to arrive at an historic moment, not only for British India but for the Indian Army Gurkha Brigade.

Long before the start of the Second World War in 1939, Indian desire for independence had been steadily growing, encouraged by the peaceful marches and demonstrations of Mahatma Gandhi. Britain's decision to declare war against Germany on India's behalf had further fanned the flame of desire for independence and of resentment at Britain's denial of it. This continued throughout the war, at times being so serious as to jeopardize Britain's ability to sustain the struggle against the Japanese in Burma.

Fortunately, the British Indian Army had, to a great extent, been unaffected by these nationalist aspirations and remained true to its salt. Indeed, without it, Britain's eventual defeat of the Japanese in Burma would not have been possible, given the prior commitment to achieve victory against Germany.

However, like Robert Atkins, Winston Churchill at the head of the wartime coalition government, whilst conceding that the grant of independence to India after the war was inevitable, envisaged a leisurely, well-ordered transfer of power as befitted the passing from its tutelage of the 'Jewel in the Imperial Crown'. In this he was supported by not only the Viceroy, Field Marshal Lord Wavell, but by the Indian Civil Service and, indeed, all old India hands such as Robert's father.

This desired course of events never came to pass; Churchill was swept from power in the 1945 election held shortly after the defeat of Germany, and a Labour government under Clement Attlee took power with a substantial majority. The new Government had entirely different ideas as to how Indian Independence should proceed – it was to happen as quickly as possible, even if that entailed the partition of India and the creation of a new Muslim nation, Pakistan, as passionately advocated by Muhammad Ali Jinnah.

This was anathema to Wavell and many other old India hands like Robert's father who forecast disaster if the process was rushed and India was partitioned along religious lines. Wavell therefore had to go, and he was replaced by a more pliant Lord Mountbatten of Burma, the military supremo of the ultimately successful Burma Campaign. This campaign had ended in August 1945 with the unconditional surrender of Japan following the dropping of atomic bombs on Hiroshima and Nagasaki, and Mountbatten, although directed to achieve Indian independence in 1948, on his own initiative advanced the date to August 1947.

Against this unsettled backdrop, Gurkha units of the British Indian Army had continued to fight the Japanese until their final surrender. When the Japanese surrender came, a number of Battalions deployed successively to French Indochina (Vietnam, Laos, Cambodia) and the Dutch East Indies (Indonesia) to combat nascent nationalist uprisings. Such deployments were designed to hold the ring until the respective colonial powers were in a position to deal with them. In the event, neither France nor Holland succeeded in doing so.

Arriving back in India, these Gurkha Battalions were soon involved in the mayhem so vividly described by Robert Atkins, as Hindus and Muslims turned on each other in a horrific orgy of slaughter. Apart from the Gurkhas, the Indian Army, with few exceptions, was comprised of Hindu and Muslim Regiments, and inevitably they were drawn into the religious conflict. Gurkhas, although ostensibly Hindu, retained many of their earlier Buddhist beliefs, so wore their

Hinduism with restraint. As a result, they became the only completely impartial upholders of law and order besides the British Garrison units still in India.

For the most part, as Robert Atkins describes, the task was just too immense and intractable for their comparatively small numbers to effectively control. After the initial shock and revulsion of witnessing the slaughter, often of whole communities across the religious divide, communities who had hitherto lived in equitable amity, Robert appears to have inured himself to such sights. Others lived with the horror of what they had witnessed until literally their dying days; it was made more galling by their inability to do very much about it. As one Gurkha officer involved explained: for a Gurkha company with 120 men, responsible for an area the size of a large English county and containing many thousands of Hindus and Muslims, the task of maintaining order and preventing communities from slaughtering each other was almost impossible. It was equally difficult to safeguard trains carrying refugees to and from the newly emergent Pakistan when faced with ambush and mass murder over hundreds of miles of track. A figure of around one million dead is generally accepted as the death toll of Partition, although the real total was probably more.

The Gurkhas themselves had their own concerns about their future: what would become of them as Nepalese citizens once India obtained her independence. Would either India or Britain still want them? One hundred and thirty thousand Gurkhas had served in the British Indian Army in the Second World War (nearly twice the total number serving in the current British Army). Their future needed to be decided.

At first, it appeared that neither India nor Britain wanted the Gurkhas, until rather late in the day it turned out that they did indeed need them. In November 1947, after Independence, a Tripartite Treaty agreed between Britain, India and Nepal ratified the employment of Gurkhas in the Indian and British armies. Six of the ten Gurkha Regiments (1st, 3rd, 4th, 5th, 8th and 9th Gurkha Rifles) would remain with the Indian Army, while four Regiments (2nd, 6th, 7th and 10th Gurkha Rifles) would transfer to the British Army.

This was obviously decided in a hurry in far-off Whitehall; apart from the retention of the 2nd Gurkhas due to lobbying by its affiliated British Regiment, the 60th Rifles, the rest were decided by some Treasury official on cost of movement grounds. The result was thoroughly illogical, as there were only two Eastern Nepal Regiments in the Brigade (7th and 10th); all the rest, with the exception of the 9th (who were mainly Brahmin), came from Western Nepal. Thus, by right, Britain should have had three Western Nepal Regiments and one Eastern Regiment.

There then came the problem of how the Gurkha soldiers themselves should be consulted about what they wanted to do. At an initial 'opt' in August 1947, Gurkhas were given the choice of serving with the Regiments going to India or those going to Britain. Although given little time for consideration, most opted to serve with Britain.

However, given the unreasonably short time they had in which to make up their minds, the results of the first 'opt' were cancelled and a further 'opt' was carried out in December 1947. This time, after three months of threats and blandishments from the newly independent India and the publication of the long-delayed terms of service from Britain, the result was very different. When it became apparent that joining the British Army would involve serving overseas in Malaya and Hong Kong, far from their Himalayan homes, Gurkhas tended to favour the new Indian Army. They had already been absent from home for the past six or seven years of war. In the end, the majority of Gurkhas opted for service with India.

An added disincentive for Gurkhas wishing to serve with those regiments destined for Britain was India's refusal to allow those in regiments destined for India to opt for service in regiments destined for Britain. Britain, on the other hand, raised no such objection to soldiers in their allocated regiments wishing to serve with India.

At this difficult time there was a barbed jest going around that the newly formed Army Education Corps' first battle honour had been the landslide Socialist victory in the 1945 General Election. The point of the joke was that Education Officers had unfettered access to virtually every soldier in their units, and using such access they had convinced many that they would be better off after the war under a Socialist government. Indeed, it was the huge service vote that propelled Labour to victory. A not dissimilar syndrome affected Gurkhas, as some Gurkha Education Officers, suitably primed by Indian agitators, convinced Gurkhas in Regiments destined for Britain that they would be better off in the new Indian Army.

This all meant that when the Regiments destined for British service eventually sailed for Malaya and Hong Kong, they were severely under strength and had to be swiftly augmented with untrained recruits. With Hong Kong under immediate threat of Chinese Communist invasion and Malaya in the grip of a burgeoning Communist insurgency, this was not the ideal way for Gurkhas to start their service as British Army soldiers.

For British officers things were, as Robert Atkins so succinctly describes, little better. Many left; some lucky ones were in Regiments destined for Britain, although cruelly many were required to make up their minds before they knew which Regiments were selected for British service. Some like Robert got back to Gurkha service having spent some time with British Regiments; others transferred permanently to them. Nearly all were demoted back to their substantive rank, so that even some wartime Brigadiers of high ability reverted to the rank of Major. It was not a happy time, although Robert clearly made the best of it.

The situation was worst of all for officers like Robert whose beloved Regiments were moving to the Indian Army. Officers' Regiments were not only their careers but their homes, and they were hugely proud not only of their Gurkhas but of their Regiment's history and customs reflected in their Regimental Depots in places such as Quetta, Dehra Dun and Abbottabad. There was always a welcome for them there amongst friends with whom they had shared their careers. Silver trophies and mementoes reminded them of their Regiment's past, as did pictures and other possessions. All this was to be handed over to strangers, and a whole way of life in peace and war came to an end.

At midnight on 14 August 1947, Captain Roger Neath of the 6th Gurkhas lowered the Union Flag for the last time above the Red Fort of Delhi, marking not only the birth of a new nation, India, but the end of the British Indian Army. Thus passed into history a magnificent body of men, all volunteers, who had fought for the Empire through two world wars and numerous smaller ones with conspicuous gallantry and elan, loyal, faithful and sadly missed.

The fledgling British Brigade of Gurkhas, despite its inauspicious start, would, as the second part of Robert's diary so clearly shows, prove itself worthy of its ancestry.

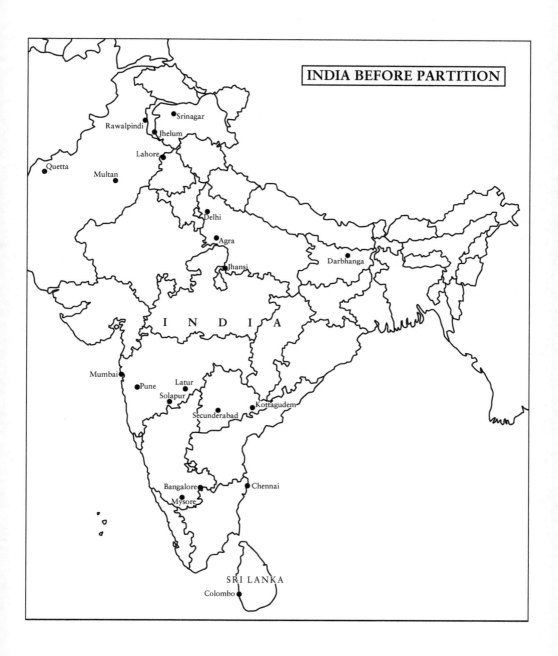

INDIA BEFORE PARTITION

Chapter 1

Family

I was born in Poona, India on 20 January 1927. I am a twin, and my mother had no idea she was going to have twins until she went into labour. I was the first born. My father was in the Indian Army and had also been born in India at Multan [now in Pakistan]. My grandfather had been the Colonel Commandant of the 15th Bengal Cavalry.

My first memories of life were of our houseboat in Kashmir and of a trout jumping on to the deck. My father retired as a Lieutenant Colonel in 1931 after commanding the 1st/15th Punjab regiment. He retired to Hayling Island, where his two elder sisters were living. Our old house is now a retired people's home.

My mother didn't like Hayling, and after three or four years we moved to Dorset. She came from a medical background: her father and brothers were doctors, and she had been a VAD (Voluntary Aid Detachment) nurse in the First World War. She later qualified as an SRN (state registered nurse) and joined the Iraqi health service. This is where she met my father, who was stationed in Baghdad at the time.

I remember my grandfather catching my brother and me smoking. He had been a surgeon and took us to look up a chimney. 'See all that soot', he said. 'That's what you are doing to your insides when you smoke.'

Geoffrey and I were sent off to prep school when we were seven and later we went to Rugby. I had decided to join the Indian Army, and in the summer of 1944 I went up to Chester for an interview to become an Indian Army cadet. The person taking the interview was Colonel Auret, late of the 10th Baluch Regiment, an old friend of my father's, so I had no difficulty in being accepted!

Shortly after D-Day (6 June 1944), I went down to London for a WOSB (War Office Selection Board) meeting, to see if I was a suitable candidate to become an officer. This took place in the Marylebone Hotel, in which we were locked in for three days. The V1 flying bombs, or doodlebugs as they were called, had just started coming over London. While at the hotel we took various aptitude tests, and one morning we were all up on the roof in our shorts doing PT, watched by a brigadier and a couple of colonels. The PT Sergeant Major was shouting 'In! Out!' as we jumped up and down doing arms and legs astride, when a doodlebug flew over and cut out more or less above us! It landed nearby with a terrific explosion, sending a great column of dust and debris into the air, but we continued with our PT as if nothing had happened!

I enlisted on 2 August 1944, had a medical and got the King's shilling. I stayed at school for another term and then went to the Indian Army cadet unit at Maidstone. We were private soldiers and did the usual square-bashing, drill, weapons training, shooting, etc. We were based at the barracks near the prison and West Station. We were not allowed out of the barracks for the first three weeks, and thereafter, we were only permitted to go three miles from the camp.

We didn't always obey this order, and once I went out to London with two or three friends. When we got back to Maidstone West Railway Station, the Military Police were at the gates checking passes, which of course we didn't have, so we went the other way towards the river, chased by a couple of MPs! We got away by climbing down the steel girders of the bridge, then ran along the riverbank and sneaked back into the camp by a back entrance through a hedge.

Chapter 2

To India

After three months' initial training we went to a pre-OCTU (Officer Cadets Training Unit) at Wrotham, where we took various tests to see if we were up to scratch, following which we had some embarkation leave and then sailed off to India in a convoy from Liverpool.

The journey wasn't much fun, and although we were cadets and could use the sergeants' mess, we were not made very welcome. We slept in cramped conditions in hammocks below deck, where you could touch three or four other hammocks from your own. The Bay of Biscay was very rough and lots of people were sick; as there were only two of us who weren't, we were given the unpleasant job of cleaning the deck. En route we stopped at Malta and Suez, and we arrived in Bombay after nearly a month at sea.

I was lucky when I arrived as I was met by a Major General who was commanding the Bombay area. He knew my father well and took me off for an excellent lunch in a hotel on the Marina Drive. When I got back to the ship, we got loaded up with our kit, packs, kitbags, etc. and marched to the railway sidings to board the train. Here I had yet another surprise when I was approached by a Punjabi Muslim who was the son of my grandfather's orderly. He wanted to be my bearer, so I took him on and arranged for him to meet me in Bangalore. It was remarkable that he knew when I was arriving and which boat I was on – a revelation of how the Indian bush telegraph works.

We stayed for a day or two in the transit camp at a place called Kalyan and then got a train which took us to Madras and on to Bangalore. We travelled in cattle trucks, but everything changed when we got to Bangalore, as we became officer cadets and lived in excellent quarters, two to a hut with a bathroom attached, and with a servant to clean our kit and look after our needs. My father, who had gone out to India again in 1942, was stationed just outside Madras at a place called Avadi, where he was running a welfare centre for the Indian troops. He came to Bangalore for a few days, and I thought he looked old and lined, but distinguished with his two rows of medal ribbons – other than the Viceroy, Lord Wavell, I think he was the only person wearing the Boer War medal.

There was an excellent club in Bangalore, the BUS (British United Services) Club, which had a good swimming pool, tennis courts and a cricket ground. There were a lot of Italian ex-prisoners of war in India and hundreds in and around Bangalore, all smartly dressed. They had been captured in various African campaigns but now wandered around at their leisure.

I broke my arm badly going on a bicycle to the rifle range at Iballur. The brake fell off into the front wheel as we were going downhill, and I landed on some rocks. The wrist was badly set and I had to have it re-broken and set again. Actually, except for the initial pain, the broken arm served me well as I didn't have to do drill or anything much physical, but watched or occasionally shouted out orders as the others marched!

I went on leave once to the Nilgiri Hills and met a very charming Indian girl who turned out to be one of the Maharaja of Mysore's daughters. After six months at Bangalore, we were commissioned and then had a few days leave in Madras with my father. We stayed in the Madras club. We all got 800 rupees as a uniform allowance which I hardly spent, as Daddy was kind enough to get most of my uniform made for me. Part of our course in Bangalore involved learning Urdu, and we had to pass an elementary exam before we were allowed to serve with Indian or Gurkha troops.

I joined the 8th Gurkha Rifles (known as the 'Shiny Eighth'). My father knew Glaxo Duncan, the Colonel Commandant, and suggested that I join it as it was probably the premier boxing regiment in the Indian Army and I was a good featherweight, having boxed for Rugby.

My first command in the Army was as O.C. (officer commanding) on the train from Madras to Quetta. The mail trains usually ran to a strict timetable, but the train I was on wasn't like that at all, even though it got to most stops on time. We halted at various places en route to take on water and get food, and I soon discovered that if I was eating in a restaurant, the guard would wait for me and would not think of starting the train until I appeared. It was a long journey from nearly the southern tip of India up to Quetta, which is not far from the border with Afghanistan. We went via Delhi, Lahore and Karachi, and the journey took four or five days, during which time I had a large first-class compartment to myself.

I took along a Dalmatian puppy which Daddy had given me; he was a lovely dog and my constant companion for the next two years. I arrived in Quetta and was quartered in the Red Square, a block of bungalows behind our Mess reserved for the junior officers. It looked out over a bleak, stony landscape typical of Baluchistan, with the Mudah Ghar mountains, north of Quetta, in the background. Our Mess was not far from the Staff College and it was a pleasant building with portraits of former Colonels hanging on walls, good Victorian polished mahogany furniture and lots of silver, with some unusual trophies and Buddhas captured or taken during the 1904 campaign in Tibet. Large stone Buddhas sat outside the front of the Mess, plus some antiquated cannon.

Quetta is at about 6,000ft above sea level and has a fairly comfortable climate, but it got very cold in the winter. It was now our regimental base. Previously, this had been in Shillong in Assam, but we had moved because of the war and the threat the Japanese had posed to eastern India.

To begin with, we learned new drill, rifle drill. This is different in many ways to that used by ordinary infantry regiments of the line. The junior officers did this under the eye of the adjutant and the *jamadar* adjutant, a Gurkha Viceroy's Commissioned officer. The war had now come to an end and we had two battalions in the Far East, one in Borneo (3rd/8th) and the other (4th/8th) in Java engaged in the fighting there. I hoped to get there and I applied to go on a jungle training course. This lasted six weeks and was held in Saugor. After an introduction, each junior officer was put into a squad alone under a corporal and worked as a rifleman. We patrolled in the jungle, made little camps, carried out mock attacks and learnt a lot of Gurkhali. You had to if you wanted a drink, food or just needed to discover what to do. The Gurkhas were charming but thought the whole affair was rather funny.

I later joined the 3rd/8th briefly after they had returned from Borneo and riot duty in Calcutta. I then spent a couple of months on the Zhob frontier, north of Quetta in the tribal territories, wild, stony, hilly country. We spent some time in Chaman on the Afghan border checking convoys coming in from Afghanistan and Persia. These were mainly camel caravans bringing in carpets and other goods to sell in Quetta and elsewhere. It was a sight from the Middle Ages. There were hundreds of camels, beautifully loaded with bags in many colours, donkeys, horses and goats, plus all manner of people in varied dress. There were Afridis, Baluchis, Pathans, Persians and many different Indian tribes; women in beautiful silk, others in black burkas, proud Waziri men with long hair and others in striking turbans. It was a wonderful sight. We checked them for weapons and admired the carpets. We visited a fort at Loralai and went out on patrols trying to seek out militant tribesmen in this lawless area. We also took part in some fairly large-scale military exercises in Nushki and Pishin, with artillery firing.

We returned to Quetta and the 3rd/8th Gurkha Rifles were disbanded. This was a rather depressing job, paying off the men and sending the regular soldiers and those who wished to remain in the Army to either the 1st or 2nd battalion. At its height, the Indian Army had over 2½ million men in arms, mostly volunteers for the duration of war. There were forty active Gurkha battalions, plus ten regimental centres and five jungle training centres.

I then went on an intelligence course to Karachi. This was mostly concerned with interpretation of aerial photographs and lasted a couple of weeks. I travelled with David Mellor, with whom I shared a bungalow. On the way back we took short leave and got off the train at Jacobabad in the Sind desert. Jacobabad is reputed to be the second hottest place in the world, with temperatures over 130°F a lot of the time. We hired camels and rode up the Bolan Pass to Quetta. Riding a camel is quite an experience. They look round at you sometimes with their long necks, and you notice their long eyelashes.

About this time, we had an outbreak of rabies in the Mess. All our dogs had been, or should have been, injected against rabies, but one of the officers, Peter Davies, who had a dachshund, hadn't had his little dog done. She got it, and so dog owners and anyone who had had contact with his dog had to be inoculated. It wasn't a pleasant injection: intra-muscular in the belly six days running. On another occasion we went out walking and a rabid pie-dog chased Bill Carey, one of the inhabitants of Red Square. He jumped on to a sweeper's bicycle and pedalled off, chased by the dog, but managed to escape. On his return, he gave the sweeper all the rupees he had on him!

Soon after I got back there was a vacancy for a staff job at the District HQ in Quetta. This was in the A Branch, and part of the time I acted as a sort of ADC to the Brigadier commanding the district. I stayed in Red Square but was driven into Quetta every morning by a driver with a small staff car. I did this job for about four months until February 1947, when I was posted to our second battalion in Secunderabad.

I also got involved with the regimental boxing team. We used to go for runs in the morning, and I did a bit of sparring with the men in the ring. This was all organized by a *subedar*, a senior Viceroy's Commissioned Gurkha Officer. We went down to Lahore for the All-India Boxing Championships, which we won. I was the team captain as I was the only British officer boxing. We won seven out of the eight All-India belts; I was the only one not to win, as I got beaten in the finals.

I enjoyed Quetta. We lived well, rode, climbed and also went out shooting mountain partridges and gazelle. We had plenty of free time but no money. The government of India didn't pay us for about six months. We didn't pay any Mess bills and were able to borrow money from Mess funds for our everyday needs and to pay our servants. This was added to our Mess bills and paid once we got our money.

We had a couple of squash courts, and one of the Khan relatives was the marker. I used to play with him a lot. We rode Army horses, and my dog loved running after my horse. We also did a lot of climbing. There were one or two fairly formidable peaks in the area. We climbed the Chiltan, which dominated Quetta, and another peak called Tukatu. These were both over 13,000ft and had snow at the top. I also did a fair amount of rock climbing in the Hannah Valley, where there was a fault in the rock cliffs with climbs over 700ft or 800ft. We had two experienced climbers from the 3rd/8th, the Thornley brothers, who showed us the ropes. Sadly, they both died climbing in the Karakorum in the 1950s.

David Mellor and I travelled down to Secunderabad together and joined the 2nd/8th Gurkha Rifles. They were a motorized infantry Battalion, part of the 43rd Gurkha Lorried Infantry Brigade in the First Indian Armoured Division. We lived in pleasant white-painted stone bungalows just outside Secunderabad.

I was still fairly innocent, and I had an extraordinary meeting with the Commanding Officer when I arrived. He was a rather fierce Scotsman who had commanded the Battalion in action in Italy and had been in a couple of Frontier campaigns before the war. I was marched into his office by the adjutant, saluted and he eyed me up and down.

'I want no nonsense from you', he said. 'No drunkenness, no gambling, getting into debt or any dirty women!' Silent pause. 'Do you understand?'

'Yes sir', I replied.

'Good. You will be all right as long as you keep your nose clean. That is all.'

I saluted and marched out – apparently that was his usual greeting to any newly arrived officer! I was put in HQ Company and made motor transport officer (MTO) and sports officer. We had about 120 vehicles in all, jeeps, 15cwt and 3-ton lorries and white scout cars, American semi-armoured vehicles. I knew nothing about cars except how to drive one, but I had a Sergeant Clerk, Chandrabahadur '(the brave moon') and a Corporal Sherbahadur ('the brave tiger'). 'Bahadur' means 'brave' and most Gurkhas have it in their given name.

Both men were old soldiers; they had been on the frontier before the war and had fought in Africa and Italy. They nursed me and helped me with my Gurkhali, which they corrected in the most helpful and respectful manner.

My dog loved jeeps and enjoyed sitting in the back. He was allowed to go everywhere – except in the dining room part of the Mess. Our routine was much the same as in Quetta: up early, wash, shave and dress and on parade at 6.30 am, breakfast; then a break from 8.30 to 10.00 and back to work until lunchtime, 12.00 or 12.30, depending on whether or not there were commanding officer's orders. In the afternoons we were virtually free, although we joined in games most afternoons with the men, hockey, basketball or volleyball.

Secunderabad was hotter than Quetta. There were some good walks in the small rolling hills behind our Mess, and I used to walk Bach, my Dalmatian, there often in the evenings.

I was gaining some idea about the maintenance of vehicles and how they worked, as demonstrated by Corporal Sherbahadur and our fitters. We had a section from IEME (Indian Electrical and Mechanical Engineers) attached the Battalion to carry out work and repairs that our drivers couldn't do themselves.

I also ran the Battalion boxing team and we won the Divisional Championships. At the end of April, I went on end of war leave. I felt rather a sham getting leave, as nearly everyone else in the battalion had been in action, in Africa, Italy or Burma. Still, I was due a month's leave and it was planned that we would trek and climb in the Eastern Himalayas. This had all been organized by the Thornley brothers, still in Quetta, who asked me to join them. We had to get passes and visas to allow us to enter Tibet and Nepal, and I applied for some extra leave so that I could join the expedition.

We left for nearly six weeks. We went first by rail to Darjeeling, where we picked up our Sherpa porters, including two women, then walked east down the Chumbi Valley. We had a wonderful view of Mount Everest from Tiger Hill. We walked through parts of Sikkim and Bhutan and eventually arrived at Gautok on the Tibetan border. We then went on up into Nepal to reach our goal, Mt Kanchenjunga. On the way the rhododendrons were magnificent, some of them huge trees covered with great fat blooms of every colour.

The higher we climbed, the smaller the trees became, many bent by the prevailing wind. There were all manner of beautiful plants and mosses until we reached the snow line. We made our base camp at a little over 15,000ft. The Sherpas all spoke Gurkhali, which we could understand, but also Bhotiya, a Tibetan dialect which of course we couldn't.

I was in charge of the base camp, and the others went on to establish another; the Thornleys were going to try for the summit. But then there was an accident. One of the Sherpas fell through a snow bridge into a deep crevasse at about 19,500ft. This brought the trip to an end. The attempts to reach the summit were cancelled and all efforts were now on bringing the injured man to safety. We had considerable difficulty pulling him up from the crevasse, since he had fallen 40 or 50 feet, breaking his leg, and was in considerable pain. The journey back was much slower as he had to be carried on a stretcher. We had morphine in our medical kit which helped deaden the pain. Bill Crace and I left the party in Gautok, and the Thornleys remained caring for the injured man, who recovered satisfactorily, although we didn't hear about this until much later. Crace and I returned to Secunderabad and the Thornleys to Quetta. They were all released later that summer.

Chapter 3

Independence and Partition

Trouble was brewing in India. Mountbatten had taken over as Viceroy, and Indian independence was being rushed through. We all thought that this would be a fairly slow process and would take two or three years. My father had predicted that there would be a bloodbath when it happened. I remember him telling me this while we were playing snooker in the Madras club one evening.

We received orders to move up to Jhansi from Secunderabad. Jhansi is in the Central Provinces and was very hot and sticky, in that period of extreme heat before the monsoon arrives.

We had marvellous quarters. I shared an old bungalow with three others: the adjutant, quartermaster and David Mellor. The bungalow, which had a big garden and compound with various outbuildings at the back, was a large airy building with a veranda at the front overlooking the garden. Inside there were large rooms, high ceilings and fans. The building was thatched. The Gurkha orderlies, all seasoned campaigners, co-opted the Indians living in the buildings behind to help clean the bungalow and work for us, otherwise they would have been moved out. We had a bevy of servants! The gardeners even watered the laterite stone path leading from the front door to our jeeps so that we wouldn't get dust on our boots!

We were now very low on British officers. There were only seven of us, so a lot of jobs were duplicated; I looked after one of the rifle companies as well as being MTO. The Gurkha Viceroy's commissioned officers, all with many years of service, were quite capable of commanding a company once the orders had been issued. The problem was their lack of understanding of English, so in a way we became the interpreters and the link between the administration and any actual military action.

Soon after our arrival in Jhansi I went on a detachment to a beautiful place called Orchha, to guard a railway bridge over the River Betwa which carried the main south/north line. If this had been blown up it would have paralysed communications. Orchha is now a tourist destination renowned for its magnificent temples and ancient buildings. We had excellent fishing, bathing in the river and good hunting in the forest. The men killed jungle fowl and peacocks, which they pulled out of the trees by their tails in the evening where they roosted.

Soon after we got back, we were woken up one night and received orders to move north immediately to join the Punjab Boundary Force and assist in quelling the civil disturbances there. We packed and left the next morning, driving in convoy up to Ferozepur, a former garrison town in the Punjab just south of the River Sutlej. The town had featured prominently in the Sikh wars of the 1840s.

As a motor infantry battalion, we prided ourselves on being able to pack everything in our vehicles and be ready to move in one hour. We left in convoy, battalion headquarters in the lead. The journey took two full days and nights of solid driving. We went via Gwalior, Agra, where I saw the Taj Mahal by night, Delhi and then Ferozepur. This became our rear echelon HQ. We arrived in the Punjab in the second week of July, when serious disturbances had already begun, Muslims from India heading north, and Hindus and Sikhs fleeing south. My bearer, Mohammed Khan, who came from the Multan district, had already left when we were in Jhansi.

The new frontier had been drawn in our area. This part of the Punjab was mainly Sikh, but there were many Punjabi Muslims as well. Most of these people were murdered, although they had previously been living together in the villages in harmony. Soon after I arrived I went to Moga, where there had been a massacre. There were dead and mutilated bodies all over the place which made me feel sick. However, it was a sight one soon got used to; in fact, one became completely hardened to these horrific sights – even rather callous.

Shortly after this I was given perhaps the most important task that I had ever had in my life. The Colonel gave me a map with various suggested routes for Hindu and Sikh refugees to follow from the north (soon to become Pakistan) to reach to India. I was told to recce the whole area and pick the best route with particular reference to water. Drinking water was crucial, and where there were no rivers or streams I was told to plan places where the engineers could install large tanks. I spent two days driving around from just south of Multan and west of Lahore down to Kasur and Ferozepur. The route was plotted, the water points agreed and this became the main route for about a million people to escape from the massacres in the Northern Punjab. The motor transport was left to Chandrabahadur, and David Mellor and I became the workhorses running the human convoys coming out. A company of Gurkhas, about 100 men, guarded or herded 50–60,000 refugees down the route. Each of our columns had a jeep, a 15cwt and 3-ton lorry per platoon and another 3-tonner for the company HQ. This carried all our stores and wireless, and we used it to pick up the lame and the old en route. These convoys lasted about ten days, and then we had a couple of days rest before we went out again.

On another occasion we went out to a train which had been attacked by a Sikh *jalta*. These were fanatical bands, often dressed in yellow, who committed terrible and bestial acts of savagery. More or less everyone on the train, Muslims going north, had been butchered. We unloaded the dead and did what we could for those still alive, not an easy or pleasant task with two or three thousand bodies, many horribly mutilated, to stack. Men had their genitals cut off, women had their breasts cut like hot cross buns, and even little babies had been slaughtered.

As Independence Day (15 August) approached, we moved up to Model Town on the outskirts of Lahore. We sent patrols into Lahore and the surrounding area and then we moved into Lahore itself, to the Gymkhana Club. Battalion HQ was in the Club, and the rifle companies lived in the grounds under canvas. C Company, under Spike Hughes who had been in the SAS during the war, was stationed in the Braganza Hotel just by Lahore Railway Station.

The 2nd/10th Gurkha Rifles were also nearby and had a difficult time with a Sikh machine gunner who was up in one of the towns overlooking the station. He was killed about an hour later after a small battle.

I was sent down to C Company to assist Spike Hughes. We had large rolls of dannert wire [coiled razor wire] separating the Hindus and Sikhs from the Muslims. We patrolled the streets round about, and the owner of the hotel, a Portuguese Indian of mixed race, was absolutely delighted to have the company based in the hotel, as we protected it from looters. A curfew had been imposed.

The 10th Dogras, an Indian regiment composed mostly of high-class Hindus, was withdrawn from Lahore after a firefight with the Additional Police, all armed and Muslim. We were visited by 'Tochi' Barker, the commander of the 43rd Gurkha Lorried Brigade, and advised not to go into the Old City except in considerable force. In riots or communal disturbances you become more or less helpless if you go into the crowd; in fact, to do so is to invite death. It is better to stand back and control from a distance, or at least from behind a barrier.

Independence Day was upon us, and I spent it in and around the Braganza Hotel. The Old City had become a bloodbath and was set alight. Fires raged, and hundreds of Hindus and Sikhs were killed. I went in with a company of Gurkhas the following day, and there was an eerie silence. Dog were sniffing and eating the corpses. A few inhabitants were still there, trying to douse the flames and create some order from the shambles that remained.

The human convoys coming out of Pakistan continued. To begin with, they were fairly jolly. They were escaping and marching towards a new life, loaded up with suitcases, carts, some animals and various belongings. A day or two's march soon sapped their vigour, however, with the dust and the merciless sun beating upon them. They couldn't stop. A column stretched for 10 or 15 miles, and soon cases were dropped, the wheels of the carts broke and the old died exhausted at the roadside. There were occasional attacks by bands of Muslims. Most of these we were able to repel – we fired a few shots and they fled – but it was difficult to police every mile of the convoy.

We saw some remarkable examples of bravery: Sikhs with drawn *kirpans* (swords) fighting off a band of attackers, like a picture out of some film set in the Middle Ages. A few shots stopped this scene!

The water points which had been planned were utterly useless, rushed upon by thousands of desperate people. They pissed and shat in the rivers and streams, and soon cholera broke out. We had a visit from our doctor and received injections to safeguard us, but he couldn't do anything to help the refugees – there were simply too many of them.

After about ten days we got to the main road, and the refugees then went off either by road or rail, although some stayed in the area and tried to remove things (to make up for what they had lost) from the north-going Muslim refugees. The situation got worse when the monsoon started. The route became a sea of mud into which dead bodies were trampled; arms, legs and sometimes heads poked out of the ground, stinking and rotting. The pie-dogs and the vultures had a field day; we used to chase the vultures in our jeeps, they were so bloated they could hardly fly. The pie-dogs became so discerning that they would rip open the dead to eat only their livers.

Of the seven British officers in the battalion, four were concerned with command and administration, the Colonel and Adjutant at Tactical Headquarters and the Second-in-Command and Quartermaster at Rear HQ dealing with administration and supply. The platoon commanders and seconds-in-command of the companies were all Gurkha Viceroy's commissioned officers, excellent, experienced soldiers, but unable to speak English. Incidentally, Sergeant Chandrabahadur and Corporal Sherbahadur, mentioned earlier, should have been given their proper Indian Army ranks of *Havildar* (Sergeant) and *Naik* (Corporal).

The situation became worse as the Colonel and Second-in-Command retired shortly after Independence, so we only had five officers left. A new Colonel, an old regular, now arrived. He had been in the RAF and had his wings up, plus the two frontier medals and the war medals, and he had been in the 8th Gurkhas since 1930. He had two bulldogs, both bitches, so my dog got along with them well.

The convoys continued, and on one a young girl gave birth to a baby in the back of my lorry. I helped with the delivery and we provided hot water and clean towels for her. I often wonder whether she and the child survived. On another occasion, coming out of the march and arriving on the main road, Lady Mountbatten and Mr Nehru were supposed to have been watching the exodus, but in fact they were cuddled together under a bridge. I was asked by the men who it was: was it the Vicereine?!

We also had visits from the press, and I took a young woman reporter, an American, up the road to where there was a pile of dead bodies. She didn't care much for the sight and departed fairly soon after!

I also took a convoy down to Delhi to get more stores and to bring up some newly repaired vehicles. Ours were getting very tired as they had all been through the war and had been driven back to India via Iraq at the end of 1945.

We travelled down the main track road via Amritsar and Jallundur. The early section of the road was a grisly sight: dead bodies on the roadside, vultures and pie-dogs, and the smell was awful for miles. In Delhi, my dog Bach (pronounced Butch) nearly gave me a heart attack. I was in the Red Fort talking to the commander of the 2nd/6th Gurkha Rifles in his office when Bach did a pee in the officer's hat, which was on the floor by his desk. Fortunately, 'Titch' Harvey didn't see this, and I left hurriedly before it was discovered! I knew him well in Malaya as a major (he had reverted to his ordinary rank then) and he was then completely bald – I often wondered why! I drove a 3-ton lorry back to Lahore.

On another occasion I was ordered to go north to escort the British resident, Colonel Webb, out of Kashmir. Again this was an interesting journey, on the main trunk road to Rawalpindi and then off up to Srinagar. Webb was a charming man, and his son, Hughie, was a good squash player. My brother had beaten him in the Public Schools Squash championship, which he won.

We also did some railway guard duty in order to stop the trains being attacked, and I went on one of these with half a company from Lahore to Multan and back. I was interested to see Multan properly, as it had been my grandfather's base and home for some years. Unfortunately, we had a nasty incident there. Three riflemen went into the bazaar, where they were murdered and their bodies thrown into a well. We had an awful time recovering the bodies, and some of the people were extremely truculent but were kept at bay by the Gurkhas with fixed bayonets.

The convoys continued through August and September, as the rains got worse and we had flooding along the Sutlej. It was discovered that the pumping stations to control the water were on the Pakistani side of the border!

When the convoys became better organized, the Air Force carried out airdrops of essential foods for the refugees. The timings were fixed on the wireless, and we would have a large clear DZ (dropping zone), which we surrounded using our own vehicles and our men standing with fixed bayonets to keep the crowds back. The problem was distribution. The weakest and neediest were always at the back of the crowd for food, whereas the strongest pushed to the front. We tried to be as fair as we could, and the Gurkha officers, the *subedars* and *jemadars*, sorted the sheep from the goats pretty well.

As the communal disturbances quietened down, there was more of a holiday atmosphere in the battalion. The Mess was now based in Lahore itself, in Gough Barracks, old colonial buildings, nice and cool, with large rooms and colonnaded verandas. We started to go out to Falletti's Hotel for dinner and once again wore dinner jackets – rather different from the dusty uniforms and the weapons we had carried constantly.

Although I was only twenty, I had been promoted to temporary Captain, so I got extra pay. Taking advantage of the more relaxed atmosphere, I drove up the Jhelum and did some fishing. I also went up to Rawalpindi fairly often; there was another Falletti's there and I knew one of the nurses who had been in Quetta, so I took her out. She was nearly thirty!

I also went to a place called Chillianwallah, where there had been a big battle in the Sikh wars. One evening we were shot at there. Obviously, someone didn't like us, and it went on nearly all night, but fortunately no one was hit. We had gone up there with a rather pleasant policeman to do some duck shooting.

The last work I did in Lahore was to go out to some villages with refugees who were returning to collect jewellery they had buried in their old homes. How they got permission to do this I never discovered. We went with some police and a Gurkha escort and dug up gold and jewels hidden in the gardens. We also came upon the most distressing sight of some Hindu girls who had been raped and kept as prisoners by their Muslim captors. They cried but declined the opportunity of coming with us. Apparently, they thought that they were tarnished goods and nobody would want them as wives anymore.

The war in Kashmir was now beginning, and on my trips to Rawalpindi I would see lorries full of Pathans with rifles and guns, all delirious and off to fight and loot the Kashmiris. An election had taken place to decide the future of the various Gurkha regiments. The 8th Gurkhas were destined for the Indian Army. Four regiments went to the British Army, the 2nd, 6th, 7th and 10th. The fighting tribes of the Gurkhas are roughly split into two halves, the Magars and the Gurungs from the West of Nepal (the 8th Gurkhas were basically a Magar/ Gurung Regiment), and the Limbus and the Rais from the East. The 2nd and 6th were Magar/Gurung regiments, and the 7th and 10th were Limbu/Rai. The men were given the chance to opt for the British regiments if they so wished. Many did, and my Sergeant Major in Malaya was in the 2nd/8th with me as a *Naik*.

In December the first of the Indian officers arrived to take over the Battalion, and our remaining officers started to leave. Colonel Spittle (ex-RAF) remained as he had opted to stay with the Indian Government. I was due for leave and left just before Christmas. I drove down to Meerut (where the Indian Mutiny started) and had Christmas there. On the way down to the train my dog Bach was killed. I had crossed the road alone, and he followed a bit later and was hit by a truck driven by a Sikh going too fast. It broke his back. I told my orderly Birbahadur to get my revolver out of the jeep and I was going to shoot him. However, he died in my arms, and we buried him by the side of the road. Looking back, it was perhaps a good way to go, and it saved him from having to spend a long time in quarantine.

Years later, I received an invitation to attend *Dushera* celebrations at 2nd/8th Gurkha Rifles in Dehra Dun; Birbahadur had become the *Subedar* Major of the Battalion. I wish I had gone but I was very busy at the time and really couldn't afford to go. Before I left India, Gandhi was assassinated. At the time I was relieved, as he had been an awful nuisance to us. Although he preached non-violence he caused the population to riot, and naturally violence ensued!

I went down to Deolali, which was a transit camp not far from Bombay. We lived in tents and there were several hundred of us waiting for a ship to take us back to England. There were a few from my term at Bangalore. I was there about a month. Deolali of course is famed as the site of a madhouse for British soldiers, hence the expression 'Deolali' [doolally], usually mispronounced!

There was a pleasant club there which not many people discovered, and a good swimming pool which I enjoyed. Eventually, I got a troopship home and arrived back in England in March 1948.

Chapter 4

Back Home

At the end of 1947 my parents had divorced. They had never been very well suited, but had behaved in a very civilized manner, keeping their arguments to themselves and not quarrelling in front of us. My mother had married her second cousin Geoffrey Marchand and was regarded as a rather scarlet woman in those days.

Daddy was living in Woodchurch in a rented cottage, and Mummy was in a rather nice house with Geoffrey just outside Barnet. My brother and I spent more time with my mother, since it was more comfortable and much more convenient for London than Woodchurch was. Geoffrey was stationed at Pirbright and was a subaltern in the Grenadier Guards. Almost as soon as I got back I caught mumps, which I had rather badly.

As soon as I was better I went to stay in Woodchurch, where old friends from the 15th Punjab Regiment were living. I was then posted to Shorncliffe, just outside Folkstone, where I did nothing except go into the town or up to London every day. Once I was orderly officer. There were dozens of officers there all waiting for a posting, and lots of other ranks all waiting to be demobbed.

I then got a rather pleasant job. I was given a small truck, a sergeant and a driver and told to go to Colchester, where I became the visiting officer at various Army cadet units and schools with cadet units in Essex and Suffolk. We didn't work very hard. I went round to various places and got to know that part of the world fairly well. We visited a unit perhaps two or three times a week, otherwise I lived in Gough Barracks (again) – but in Colchester.

I was next posted to the 1st Battalion of the Royal Fusiliers in Germany. I enjoyed my time with them. I was a platoon commander, and most of the time was spent training fairly raw soldiers. We did the usual things, drill, shooting and field craft. I had with me the excellent Sergeant Oakman, who became the Regimental Sergeant Major before he retired and whom I met years later in the City when he was the Beadle of the Carpenters' Livery Company. I remember he looked after me extremely well when I dined there one evening. When I telephoned to thank him and asked him to come out for a drink, he laughed and said he'd love to, but that the drink was much better at the Livery Hall (which it was) – so I went there instead!

We had a very interesting and charming company commander, James Hope-Johnson, known as 'Hopeless-Johnson'. He was mad about shooting, hawking and painting. He had a dog called York, an old English pointer, and sitting on a log on his desk was a goshawk! When he was not riding, hunting or hawking, he painted in oils, very well indeed.

Soon after I arrived I went on a route march and exercise with the company and we took over a German farm on the outskirts of the Harz mountains. The officers lived in the farm house and the men in various buildings around the farmyard. After experiencing austerity in England, I was amazed at the food the Germans had: hams hanging from the ceiling, milk and cream galore. We ate well there ourselves!

One day, we had made a bonfire in a quarry nearby and were sitting round it. Suddenly shots started going off. Our fire had been built on top of some ammunition that had been dumped or hidden by the Germans. It was very frightening – even more so when Hope-Johnson ordered, 'Robert, put the fire out!' I did this by scattering the logs all over the place and raking the embers away. Luckily, not a soul was hit, although I burnt my boots and trousers and got pretty hot as well.

We were based at Iserlohn on the edge of the Ruhr and had a pleasant social life there. We went around to various regiments where we had friends, rode and shot; and when it got colder, there was good skating on a lake nearby and we went up to Winterberg to ski. There were no ski lifts, but it was fun.

I applied for a regular commission and in June 1949 went back to England for a Regular Commission Board. We did various aptitude tests and exercises and had to give lectures to those present, with the selection board looking on. Anyway, I passed with a good grade.

In the autumn I went on a detachment as an assault troop commander to Lübeck with a cavalry regiment, the 15th/19th Hussars. We had a very good Mess on the river which was virtually part of the sea looking over the city, which had been very badly bombed during the war. We carried out patrols along the frontier between Russia and Eastern Germany. I spent Christmas there; it was very cold, the rivers froze and we had excellent skating. Our garden ran down to the water's edge and we had braziers heating hot toddy to refresh us as we skated at night.

I then went back to the Royal Fusiliers in Berlin. Again, much of Berlin had been flattened during the war, but we had a good time there. There were (are) some excellent nightclubs on the Kurfürstendamm which we patronized whenever we could. Life was much the same: a bit of drill, training and a fair amount of free time.

The Korean War had just begun, and two of us were posted to a camp in England to join drafts going there. I had a couple of weeks of embarkation leave which I spent mostly with my parents. Then I went up to Otley in Yorkshire for a couple of weeks before going to Liverpool to sail off to Korea. Almost everyone going, the soldiers and some of the officers, were reservists who had been recalled to the colours.

We stopped at Suez, where one man who was very drunk fell off the gangplank and was killed when he hit the side of the dock. We also stopped at Aden and Colombo. I met my cousin Kathy there, who was married to a shipbroker and had been an announcer on Radio Ceylon during the war. She was Uncle Douglas's daughter and a very good-looking woman. We went to their house and also visited Mount Lavinia and the zoo.

When we got to Singapore, I received orders to disembark and join the Brigade of Gurkhas. My father had organized this! In a way I regretted not going to Korea, but I would probably have been killed. Of the three others I shared a cabin with two were killed; one was Phil Curtis (he got a VC with the Glosters), and the other was Terry Waters GC, who was killed in captivity by the Koreans. When I got to Singapore I was put in a transit camp for a day or two and then moved to Johore Bahru.

Part II

A Malayan Diary

Introductory Commentary

Brigadier Christopher Bullock

The surrender of British and Imperial troops in Singapore on 15 February 1942 represented the low point of the war for Britain and for Winston Churchill. In his history of the Second World War Churchill described the surrender as 'the worst disaster and the largest capitulation in British history'. At least Dunkirk, although a military disaster, had been redeemed by the almost miraculous rescue of the Army from the beaches.

As news of the extent of the disaster spread through the Empire, nearby members such as Burma (whose turn would come shortly), Australia, New Zealand and even India realized how vulnerable they were. If an Imperial army of 100,000 men in the supposedly impregnable fortress of Singapore could capitulate to a Japanese force little more than half its size, what hope was there?

Amidst this general gloom and despondency there flickered a continuing faint flame of resistance against what seemed the irresistible power of Imperial Japan. Deep in the jungles of Malaya, the rather unlikely warriors of 'The Malayan People's Anti-Japanese Army' (MPAJA) continued to confront the invaders. The background to these events needs to be explained.

Dutch traders in the sixteenth century were the first Europeans in Malaya and dominated certain areas of it such as Penang, but Britain's East India Company was founded in 1600, and by 1894 Britain, through a series of fairly gentlemanly agreements with various Malay Sultans, had taken control of the whole peninsula, with the inconvenience of only one small war. The Sultans were left to rule their areas of control such as Johore and Perak much as they had always done. Singapore had already been colonized by Sir Stamford Raffles.

The Malays, a charming, graceful people, although acknowledging British overall control, had not the slightest intention of changing their traditional ways and customs under their Sultans. If the British wanted labour to tap the trees in their newly established rubber plantations or wash for tin in their ugly opencast mines, they could find it elsewhere; Malays would certainly not be doing it.

This the British duly did, bringing in Tamils from Ceylon (Sri Lanka) and India to work as rubber-tappers, and Chinese from Southern China to work the tin mines and act as clerks, book-keepers and small entrepreneurs. These Chinese, as is their style, worked hard and prospered in Malaya, as they had earlier done in Singapore, much to the disdain of the Malays, who resented them.

Always mindful of their mother country, the Straits Chinese (so called after the Straits of Malacca) hated the Japanese, who in the 1930s had conquered large swathes of their country, inflicting great cruelty on the population. The setting up of a Japanese puppet state in Manchuria was a standing affront. They also became aware of the growing conflict within China between Chiang Kai-shek's Nationalists and Mao Zedong's Communists and tended to identify with one or the other.

The Malayan Communist Party (MCP) aligned itself with Mao Zedong and accordingly nurtured the rather improbable aim of ridding Singapore and Malaya of the British and setting up a 'Dictatorship of the Proletariat' – regardless of the fact that the ethnic Malays were totally uninterested in any such notion. However, when the hated Japanese invaded Malaya, the Malayan Communist Party immediately offered their help to the British. With the campaign in Malaya going very badly, this offer was gratefully accepted. Lieutenant Colonel Spencer Chapman set up a special training school and armed and equipped the personnel the MCP provided.

As defeat in Malaya loomed, the MCP now became the MPAJA and, helped and supplied by Force 136, co-ordinated by Spencer Chapman, kept the spark of resistance alive. How much of a threat they posed to the Japanese is debatable; they were probably only a minor irritant, and their brave members were savagely eliminated when captured. But it was important that they were continuing to resist, and with Burma now in Japanese hands and India's North-Eastern provinces threatened, the MPAJA's lonely battle was significant.

Once the Japanese surrendered and the war was over, British settlers in Malaya, who had been imprisoned by the Japanese in often appalling conditions, happily emerged to take up their previous occupations as Government officials, District Officers, managers of rubber plantations and tin mines, and businessmen. They expected their lives to return to the pleasant, slightly laid-back style so well described in Somerset Maugham's short stories.

The MPAJA had different ideas. Having gone through the charade of being lauded for their wartime achievements, with their leader Chin Peng having been appointed OBE, they briefly performed guard duties and then disappeared into the jungle, changing the 'J' in their title to 'B' to become the 'Malayan People's Anti-British Army' or, as the British security forces called them, 'Communist Terrorists' (CTs). They reverted to their original aim of driving the British out of Malaya and taking it over themselves.

Their tactics closely mirrored those of Mao Zedong. First, they aimed to control areas of countryside (both jungle and cultivation), driving the security forces back into the towns and creating liberated areas which they could then deny to the security forces. As these areas of control expanded, the surrounding towns would be starved of supplies so that they too would eventually succumb. A similar tactic was used by the Communists in China and Vietnam with evident success.

Meanwhile, the British Government of Malaya was living in something of a fool's paradise. Belatedly, they had realized that through the efforts of Force 136 the original MPAJA had received large quantities of weapons, ammunition and equipment, and this had been augmented by what they had captured from the defeated Japanese. The British offered a reward for the return of weapons, and some 5,000 were surrendered (while 7,000 rewards were claimed!). However, since the authorities had no idea how many weapons were in the MPAJA's possession they had no means of knowing what proportion had been handed in. It turned out to have been a very small one. The retained weapons were soon being used to murder rubber plantation and tin mine managers, ambush police and military vehicles, derail trains, attack police stations and terrorize the local population.

Gradually, the authorities came to appreciate that after recently losing Malaya to the Japanese they would soon lose it again to a Communist insurgency unless the most urgent and vigorous steps were taken to prevent it.

Initially, the Government of Malaya was ill-equipped to confront this escalating threat. The mainly Malay police force was very much a peacetime constabulary and neither equipped nor trained to confront well-armed, experienced insurgents. The Army comprised seven Gurkha battalions (but as we have seen, many of their number were virtually untrained recruits) and three British battalions. Co-operation between Police Special Branch and the Army was poor; the Police were reluctant to give information to the Army for fear of compromise, and vice versa. Energetic and dynamic leadership was required, and Robert's diary touches on this.

Fortunately, it was a case of 'Cometh the hour, cometh the man', and this was in the form of Lieutenant General Sir Harold Briggs, a previous Divisional Commander in General Slim's victorious Fourteenth Army in Burma. In 1950 he was appointed Director of Operations in Malaya and soon realized that formidable as the CTs were, they relied to a vulnerable extent on the Min Yuen, the numerous Chinese farmers and squatters living on the edge of the jungle. Terrified by or sympathetic to the CTs, they provided them with food, medicine and many other necessities. Briggs saw that if the

Min Yuen could be concentrated into defended villages and obliged to observe dawn-to-dusk curfews, the CTs would be forced into the open, making them easier targets for the security forces.

This ambitious plan required much determination; not only was it a massive logistical undertaking, but the propaganda wing of the CTs made sure to publish ample coverage of police and troops burning existing villages, and pictures of screaming mothers with babies at their breasts being herded into the new fortified ones. There was massive international outrage and much unhappiness in Britain. Nevertheless, Briggs persisted with his plan, although all the pressures it caused led to a decline in his health, and he died before its success could slowly become apparent.

As Briggs had foreseen, cutting the CTs off from their infrastructure forced them to come into the open and contact sympathizers to try and keep supplies coming in. In so doing they laid themselves open to interception by the security forces. They were also obliged to try and grow food in jungle clearings near to their camps. This made them vulnerable to observation by Auster light aircraft and air photography. The interpreted photographs were sent to the combined operations rooms, who could then alert the nearest units.

Briggs also did much to ensure that the Army's equipment and weaponry were suited to prolonged jungle warfare. In achieving this, he was building on the representations of 22nd Guards Brigade, who had come to Malaya as an emergency reinforcement. They were appalled at being expected to spend weeks in the jungle wearing hobnailed boots which fell to bits, carrying large heavyweight radio sets, eating totally unsuitable rations and being armed with wartime weaponry. As Guardsmen, they tended to have influential contacts, and matters soon improved. Special canvas jungle boots appeared, as did better and lighter radio sets and more suitable rations, whilst the Lee Enfield short No 5 Rifle replaced the old No 4, and the light M1 American semi-automatic carbine and the Australian Owen sub machine gun delivered greatly increased firepower.

Nevertheless, despite all these improvements, the CTs still held the initiative until the arrival of General Sir Gerald Templer, who took over as the High Commissioner when Sir Henry Gurney was ambushed and killed by the CTs. Vitally, he also took over as Director of Operations from the then terminally ill General Briggs. He thus became in essence military and civil supremo, and this most brave, energetic and intelligent man was determined to use all his considerable powers to turn the tide against the CTs.

General Templer soon grappled briskly with inefficiencies in the campaign. He set up 'Joint Operations Rooms', where civil authorities, police and the military worked closely together, sharing information, allocating resources and planning joint operations. The whole of Malaya was split into colour-coded areas of black, grey and white. Black were CT-dominated areas, grey areas were disputed, and white indicated the areas where CTs had been eliminated. Under his dynamic direction, black areas soon became grey and grey, white, as a result of highly successful operations like those described so vividly in Robert's diary.

By late 1958 the terrorist remnants had been largely driven over the border into Thailand, and in 1960, after twelve years of tenacious campaigning and the successful attrition of Communist terrorists by the security forces, the Malayan Emergency was declared over. A grand Victory Parade marking its successful conclusion was held in Kuala Lumpur, and a contingent of the 6th Gurkha Rifles was among the many worthy participants celebrating the occasion. In one of the few successful counter-insurgency operations of the Cold War the campaign had seen British and Commonwealth Forces defeat a Communist revolt and allowed Malaya to achieve independence, peace and prosperity.

The key components of that victory had been the combination of political, social and economic policies designed to work alongside a successful military strategy, all planned and directed, successively, by Generals Briggs and Templer. Those policies – including a well-developed 'Hearts and Minds' campaign – eventually won the support of the civil population. The resettlement of some 400,000 people into 500 new villages that severed the lifeline of support for the terrorists had been a key component of the Government's strategy. Additionally, hard-learned jungle warfare skills honed by the security forces eventually denied jungle sanctuary to the terrorists and allowed them to be systematically eliminated.

Over 11,000 people died as a direct result of the Emergency. This grim total included at least 500 Commonwealth soldiers and 1,300 Malay soldiers and police, men and women; many more were wounded, while 2,500 civilians also lost their lives.

The terrorist death toll can only be imprecisely calculated, but certainly over 6,000 CTs were directly killed on operations by the Security Forces. Additionally, a further 4,000 terrorists were wounded, captured or surrendered. By the end of the campaign the elimination of communist terrorists within the Malay Peninsula was total.

The 6th Gurkha Rifles' Roll of Honour includes the names of fifty-nine officers and men killed during the Emergency, while a significant further number were wounded – all in armed contact with the enemy. In return, the Regiment accounted for at least 400 terrorists killed, as well as making a major contribution to their wider attrition. It was a fine record.

* * *

Robert's high regard for his Commanding Officer, Lieutenant Colonel Walter Walker, comes through clearly in his diary. Although there were many inspirational British and Gurkha Commanding Officers, Walter Walker was certainly one of the best known and most successful. He had commanded the 4th Battalion of the 8th Gurkhas towards the end of the war in Burma. At that time the Japanese were fighting desperately to hold the mountainous Pegu Yomas area of central Burma. The 4th/8th Gurkha Rifles held a vigorous Japanese counter-attack at bay, and the demanding nature of the fighting was demonstrated by Rifleman Lachhiman Gurung's distinguished and gallant conduct, earning him the Victoria Cross. Then, after India gained Independence, Walter Walker commanded the 1st Battalion of the 6th Gurkha Rifles where he met Robert, who had also originally belonged to the 8th Gurkhas. Walker went on to command the 99th Gurkha Brigade in Malaya during the war against the CTs and then to command 17th Gurkha Division, also in Malaya, once the Emergency was over. He further assumed the mantle of Major General Brigade of Gurkhas and in that capacity did much to halt Ministry of Defence plans to reduce Gurkha numbers in the wake of the CTs' defeat. Later, General Walker, still in command of 17th Gurkha Infantry Division, was appointed the successful and dynamic Commander British Forces in Borneo as the campaign against Indonesian confrontation unfolded, involving the British Army in a further jungle campaign that drew on many lessons learnt during the Malayan Emergency.

Robert's description of his time in the jungle gives a clear picture of the sheer hard graft of jungle operations: endless hours lying motionless in ambush, soaked by rain and plagued by mosquitoes, always remaining alert for the tug on the vine from a sentry that would herald the terrorists' approach. Then there were the meticulously defended CT camps, where the slightest sound would alert an enemy whose animal caution and cunning were renowned.

Much time was spent just slogging through the bamboo and thorn of the jungle, generally on an empty stomach and with 70lbs on each soldier's back, amid constant danger from potentially lethal wild animals, snakes, scorpions and leeches, quite apart from all the variety of tropical diseases to be caught from infected water and mosquito and mite bites – and always the threat of a ruthless enemy.

Robert's diary gives a true feel for all of this. Most striking, however, are his encounters with the CTs, fascinatingly described. Given that many officers and men involved in the Emergency never encountered a CT, the number and variety of Robert's 'contacts' not only mark his courage and leadership but also his tactical skill and that of his Gurkhas in bringing the CTs to battle.

Some of these 'contacts' were large-scale, such as the one for which he was awarded the Military Cross, but there were many smaller 'contacts' that required as much or more skill to corner an elusive and dangerous enemy. The continuing danger posed by the CTs was demonstrated not least by the high casualty rate among British and Gurkha officers, who invariably led from the front and paid a grim price for their leadership. There can have been few if any officers involved who saw as much action as Robert.

Newly married, Robert's young wife, Anabel, must have been uncertain each time Robert left her for an operation whether or not she would see him again; a tremendous strain for them both so early in their marriage.

This is the diary of a very special Gurkha infantry officer.

Malaya Timeline

1786	Penang ceded to the East India Company by the Sultan of Kedah
1819	Singapore Island leased to the East India Company
1824	Malacca transferred to British control. Singapore leased in perpetuity
1826	Penang, Singapore and Malacca known as The Straits Settlements
1867	The Straits Settlements become a British Crown Colony
1870s	First trials of rubber trees
1896	Federated Malay States formed from Selangor, Perak, Negeri, Sembilan and Pahang
1904	The unfederated States of Kelantan, Kedah, Terengganu and Perlis accept British advisers
1914	Johor accepts British advisers
1941	Japan invades Malaya
1942–5	Malaya and Singapore are occupied by the Japanese
1948–60	Communist insurgency causes 'Emergency' to be declared
1957	Federation of Malaya achieves independence
1959	Singapore achieves independence
1963	Malaysia formed

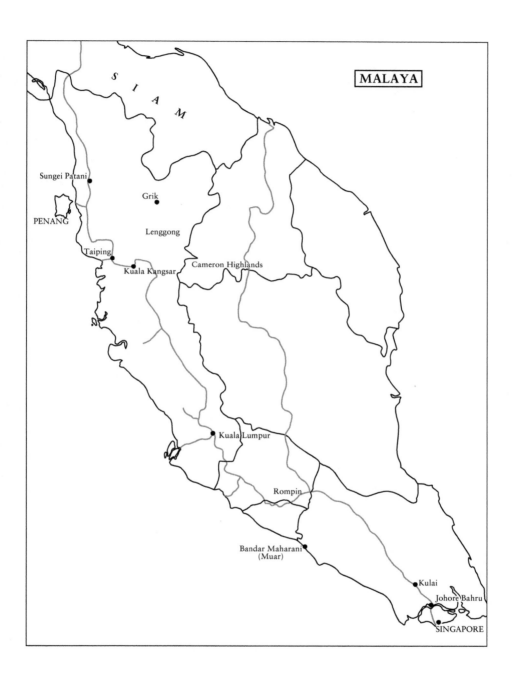

MALAYA

SIAM

Sungei Patani

Grik

PENANG

Lenggong

Taiping

Kuala Kangsar

Cameron Highlands

Kuala Lumpur

Rompin

Bandar Maharani
(Muar)

Kulai

Johore Bahru

SINGAPORE

Chapter 1

To Malaya

In October 1950 I was in Johore Bahru, working as the Battalion intelligence officer based in the police station which looked over the Straits to Singapore. We had a big ops room shared with the police special branch. These were mostly Chinese-speaking police officers and they were the main producers of operational intelligence, derived from the interrogation of SEP (surrendered enemy personnel) and other communist suspects.

I spent most of my day on and off the wireless, getting information from the various patrols, then coordinating their positions on the map and keeping the commanding officer up to date. The police produced information on terrorist incidents – murder, burning buses, shots at the train, etc., so we got a good overall picture of what was happening in our area. This was all entered on the main operations map.

The Malayan Emergency been declared in June 1948. This was the result of a series of major attacks carried out by the MRLA (Malayan Races Liberation Army) with the aim of paralysing the British administration and taking over the country.

Large numbers of Chinese had fought against the Japanese after they occupied the country in 1942. During the war the British supplied these Chinese with arms by air, so they had built up considerable reserves of weapons and ammunition, which were now being used against us. Most of these Malay Chinese were communists and were encouraged by China. Malaya was a hotbed of communism, the local population being mainly poor labourers. The rich in Malaya, largely British or European plantation owners or managers, were very, very rich indeed compared to the rubber-tappers and agricultural workers on these estates.

Business in the towns was largely controlled by Chinese and some Indian businessmen. Many of them would have been happy to see us go, largely because the Malayan Civil Service (MCS) was very much biased in favour of the weaker, charming but indolent indigenous Malays.

There was very much more to the communist threat than chasing, ambushing and killing the terrorists in the jungle. There were very many active supporters living in towns and villages and supplying the hard core with food, medical supplies and information, although this Min Yuen supply route had been curtailed to some extent by the Briggs plan.

General Briggs (ex-Indian Army) was the first Director of Operations in Malaya. His plan was ruthless; sensible from a military point of view, but unpopular. All Chinese farmers and labourers were resettled within their own areas. Each village was surrounded by a high barbed-wire fence, and entry and exit were controlled by armed Malay police. Searches were made to stop the inhabitants taking any supplies out. At night the perimeter of the town or village was lit.

Numerous extra police and resettlement officers were employed on short-term contracts by the government. A lot of these were ex-Palestine Police or senior non-commissioned officers who had not settled into civilian life after the war.

The brunt of the hunting out and destruction of the MRLA devolved on the Brigade of Gurkhas. Six active battalions were based in Malaya and two in Hong Kong. Most of the Gurkhas were already skilled jungle fighters after their experiences in Burma, Indonesia and other parts of South-East Asia. There were, of course, also many battalions of British infantry, cavalry and supporting troops. Most of the soldiers were national servicemen, not regulars like the Gurkhas. At the height of the Emergency nearly 125,000 troops were deployed in Malaya and Singapore against a hard core of about 10,000 communist terrorists in the jungle – with, of course, the backing of the Min Yuen and other sympathizers.

To understand the narrative, it is necessary to know how a Gurkha battalion was made up. There were usually thirteen British or Gurkha commissioned officers per battalion. There was then a second tier of Gurkha officers, mostly platoon commanders, who held a different commission. They were known as King's Gurkha Officers (KGO), later Queen's Gurkha Officers (QGO). A battalion has six companies, each of about 100–120 men. The commanding officer (1), a Lieutenant Colonel, is the chief executive and is assisted by a second-in-command (2), an adjutant (3), his main staff officer, and an intelligence officer (4). The quartermaster (5) runs the supplies for the battalion, i.e. food, clothing, arms and ammunition, etc. The MTO, Motor Transport Officer (6), runs the battalion's transport, and the RMO, Regiment Medical Officer (7) looks after its health. The RMO is an officer from the Royal Army Medical Corps and probably a qualified doctor, usually posted to a battalion for a three-year period. These services are all included in HQ Company.

Support Company was commanded by a captain or major and consisted of three platoons providing local support for the battalion. In the jungle in Malaya it was used as an additional rifle company. The company consisted of:

The Anti-Tank Platoon
The Mortar Platoon (3″ mortars)
The Machine Gun Platoon, armed with Lewis machine guns

Each platoon was commanded by a Gurkha officer (QGO) or a sergeant.

The four rifle companies (A, B, C and D) were the fighting teeth of the battalion, each commanded by a captain or major, together with a Gurkha captain as second-in-command. Each company had three platoons commanded by a Gurkha officer or a sergeant. There are three sections per platoon, with a corporal in charge of each. The main weapon of each section is a Bren LMG (light machine gun) capable of firing 650 rounds per minute.

A newly arrived subaltern, a lieutenant or second lieutenant, was generally appointed company officer to one of the rifle companies to learn the ropes. His most important asset was a good working knowledge of Gurkhali, as all business was conducted in that language, except for drill orders which were in English.

Chapter 2

December 1950–November 1951

There was trouble in Singapore in November 1950, inter-racial riots caused by the parents of a Muslim girl called Maria Hertogh, who had been adopted by a Dutch/Indonesian Christian family. We moved two companies in to quell these riots, and the troublemakers were quickly dispersed by Gurkhas advancing with bayonets fixed. North of JB (Johore Bahru) there was a hotspot called Kulai, a village 19 miles upcountry. This was a favourite place for terrorists to shoot up the night mail train and occasionally derail it. I was subjected to an ambush on the road near Kulai but drove through it in my Dingo armoured car. I spent Christmas 1950 in Kulai with the OCPD (Officer Commanding Police District), James MacNab, later to become the MacNab of MacNab. His house was on a hillock overlooking the village and at night it sometimes became the target for a terrorist sniper. We had sandbags all around the house above chair/bed level and turned down the lights at night to lessen the chances of being seen.

During the next two or three months we had several contacts with the enemy, and I was involved with two of these. I was ambushed on the edge of a rubber estate when out with a patrol. We came under heavy fire from a couple of Bren guns and had three Gurkha riflemen wounded. After a fierce exchange of fire we advanced, and the terrorists withdrew into a swampy area which made the trail difficult to follow. We believe we killed or wounded some, as there were several substantial blood trails, but we were unable to recover any bodies.

On another occasion a terrorist camp located in a similar area was attacked. It was strenuously defended, and after a short battle, the terrorists retreated. One dead enemy was left, and one British officer was wounded in the attack. We also patrolled the Kota Tinggi Peninsula without much success, but I was fortunate enough to see a baby rhino and mother at close quarters in a small clearing on the edge of a mangrove swamp.

May 1951

In May 1951 I moved up to Bahau in Negri Sembilan. I was posted to understudy Gil Hickey, who commanded a detachment at Rompin. This was small village close to the main north/south railway and was the last outpost before a swathe of jungle between Johore and Negri Sembilan. Gil was going on leave to get married, and the idea was that I was to take over while he was away.

Our camp was a tented one, except for a small wooden house which Gil and I lived in. We had a shared bedroom, sitting room, shower and one room which was used as the company office, wireless and ops room. The camp was on the edge of a rubber estate.

The estate was run by a young Englishman called John Carter, who was living with a Malay woman. He was a fairly constant visitor and often came over in the evening for a drink or some supper. One evening, he regaled us with the story of how he had been ambushed some months previously. He had driven down a track on the estate and found it blocked by fallen tree and a party of terrorists in waiting, who fired at his car. He backed his vehicle, fortunately an armoured Ford, and drove off on to another estate road which allowed him to escape. It had been a very unpleasant experience.

A day or two later, we heard shots south of us on the estate. B Company had a patrol in the jungle in this direction, so we opened the wireless to see what was afoot. Presently the north/south mail train could be heard climbing the hill up into Rompin. It stopped momentarily at the station, a few hundred yards down the road, and then continued its journey north.

A minute or two later, a white-faced, mud-splattered Carter ran into our house panting, missing one shoe and without the glasses that he normally wore.

'I have been ambushed again', he gasped.

'Where?' we asked.

'In the same place.'

The trouble was that Gil didn't know where this same place was! It took a minute or two to discover its whereabouts, then a platoon was sent down to track and follow up the terrorists.

We heard Carter's story. As usual, he had driven down to see the tappers at work, fortunately again in his armoured Ford. The estate road was again blocked, in a slightly different place this time, so that it was not possible for him to drive off and escape. Another tree was then felled behind him, so he was trapped. There were fifteen or twenty armed and uniformed terrorists with red stars on their caps surrounding him. They fired at his car, but without effect. Then they produced a can of petrol, doused the engine, set fire to it and stood back to watch.

Carter decided he would rather be shot than roasted alive and made a dash for it. He opened the car door and ran. His exit was unexpected. He jumped down into a little stream and tripped over a root in the water (his glasses had been broken when he ran into the barricade). Shots whistled overhead, and he rushed on, followed by a hail of bullets. Luckily the enemy fire was inaccurate, and miraculously he was not hit. As he ran through the rubber estate, he saw the upcountry mail train chugging its way slowly up the hill towards Rompin. He ran frantically and hurled himself on to the moving train. He had escaped.

I went down to the scene of this ambush shortly afterwards with the platoon that was sent down to follow up the bandits. The men spread out as they got out of their armoured lorries and walked towards the jungle edge. Carter's car was a smouldering wreck, and all around the rubber trees were spattered with bullet holes and bleeding white latex, showing how lucky he had been not to be hit.

July 1951

Gil went on leave to get married at the end of July, and I was then in temporary command of the detachment. B Company's second-in-command was a very experienced Gurkha officer, Captain (QGO) Manu Gurung MBE, MC. He was a veteran of two campaigns on the North-West Frontier as well as three and a half years fighting in Burma. He was forty-one, which to most of us in those days was fairly ancient! Most of the Gurkha riflemen were teenagers. He had been in Wana (on the NW Frontier) at the same time as my father, when he was commanding the 1st Battalion 15th Punjab Regiment (1930–31).

Also under command at Rompin was a troop of the 13th/18th Hussars who had four large Daimler armoured cars equipped with two-pounder guns and Lewis heavy machine guns, plus two Dingo scout cars. This troop was used mainly for escort duty to and from Bahau, and also as a show of force on the various local rubber estates.

August 1951

Soon after I took over, this troop was ambushed by a terrorist gang on the corner of the Rompin/Bahau road by the turning up to Kok Foh Estate. It happened in mid-morning and only about three miles from our camp. A mine had been planted in the roadside and it was detonated by the first vehicle. The convoy then came under heavy fire from the jungle-clad embankment overlooking the road.

The young troop leader, a second lieutenant just out from England, returned fire with 2-pounder shells and machine guns and then withdrew, unfortunately leaving one upturned vehicle fully armed. He returned to my base with the dead and wounded that his sergeant had retrieved.

Obviously, we had heard explosions and heavy firing, and I put the stand-to platoon on readiness to go out. I reported to the Colonel on the wireless and he decided to send a company down from Bahau to investigate. My stand-to platoon was to be sent into the jungle immediately, striking northwards to act as a cut-off.

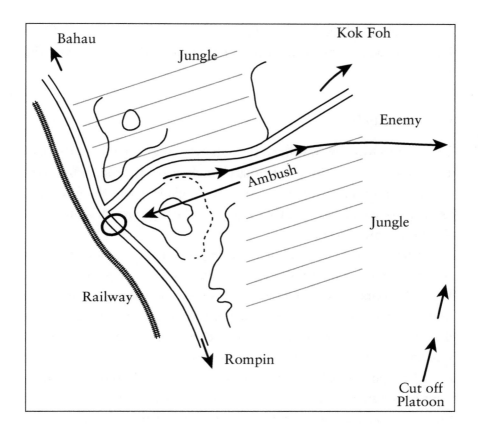

I dealt with the wounded. A Chinese liaison officer had been seriously wounded in the stomach and unfortunately died. One BOR (British Other Rank) was killed and two others wounded. Three .303 rifles were lost, captured by the enemy, and one vehicle was destroyed. The young officer in charge was sent back to England.

This had been a well-planned and cleverly executed attack. Kok Foh estate was at the end of the road where the ambush had taken place. It was an oil palm estate and very overgrown. The owner was a large, fat and rather pleasant middle-aged Chinese called Ah Lee. He also owned another smaller rubber estate near the corner of the Bahau/ Kok Foh road. He was unable to work Kok Foh, which had become too dangerous for him and his workforce. The terrorists constantly demanded protection money from him, and they also ordered him to give them food and supplies, which would have landed him in trouble.

He offered to sell me Kok Foh for about $1,200 Malay – about £160! He was, however, able to work his rubber estate, which was nearer the main road.

September 1951

The road to Kok Foh was lined by high overhanging banks with rocks and thick secondary jungle. Primary jungle consists of huge old trees with a high canopy, whereas secondary jungle is where the forest has been cut back and regrown. Consequently, the trees are not so high and the undergrowth is thicker

Acting on Ah Lee's information about Kok Foh, I decided to comb the area and set up a series of small ambushes on the edge of the road. We had a contact and killed two terrorists, one of whom shot at me and hit me in the leg from above on one of the steep banks. It turned out that she was a young woman armed with a .38 revolver, although this was not discovered until the bodies were taken to the local police for identification. Luckily, my wound wasn't severe, although the bullet went in one side of the leg and came out the other. It had only grazed the shinbone, and the wound healed up in a few days. I had an X-ray in the local hospital late that evening.

On another occasion an ambush was laid on the edge of the Chinese estate owner's rubber plantation, and Lance Corporal Jitaram chased and shot two more of the enemy, He was later awarded the Military Medal. This was the first time I had made a recommendation for a medal.

When we went into the jungle, each person wore jungle-green trousers and a long-sleeved shirt. Under this we wore boxer shorts and a vest. Our jungle boots were made of canvas with rubber soles; they came nearly up to the knee and were fastened with metal clips like skating boots. We also wore a jungle-green hat which was reversible. On patrol we turned this inside out to reveal our regimental sign, a Roman VI, in orange.

You wore a webbing belt and crossover straps, on which were two pouches and a small haversack. The latter contained mess tins and eating irons, and washing kit including a small towel. In the pouches you carried ammunition, grenades, a spare magazine for the Bren gun, forty rounds of .303 for those with rifles (Lee Enfield Mark 5 in those days) or spare filled magazines for those with M1 carbines or Sterling sub machine guns. On patrol all weapons were loaded ready for action with safety catches applied. You each carried a field dressing in case you were wounded, and this was held in a special pouch in your trousers on the front of the left thigh.

On your back you carried a large pack, on the outside of which was your waterproof poncho. Inside were four tins of rations, a light blanket, a jumper, a spare warmer shirt, spare socks and gym shoes. Section, platoon and company commanders also carried a compass and a map case. The men had a *kukri* each, either on the belt or the big pack. This classic Gurkha knife/machete was used as a maid of all work, for chopping wood, cutting sticks etc., as well as a personal weapon.

The whole lot weighed about 70lbs, plus the weight of your weapon, 8lbs for a rifle, more for the Bren and less for a carbine or sub-machine gun. The pack got lighter as you ate your rations. After four days out you got an airdrop which replenished your food, and then the pack became heavy again.

The signaller (one per platoon) carried a wireless set, and we also had one medical pack per platoon with a supply of morphine and penicillin. The usual routine in the jungle was a 'stand-to' at first light and again in the evening. We started moving after the morning meal, which consisted of cold curry and a cup of tea. We marched or patrolled for an hour, rested for ten minutes, and then moved off again. Generally we moved in single file, and the main responsibility and danger lay with the leading scouts. These riflemen, often teenagers, took it in turns to move forward, halt and move forward again. The leading section commander (a corporal or lance corporal) travelled just behind them, supported by the section Bren gun.

When a new track was found or something suspicious was seen, we halted. Little patrols of two or three men were sent out sideways and forwards for 100 yards or more to see if there was any movement. We never crossed an obstacle (a small river etc.) without support from an LMG, or moved into a defile without sending a patrol up each side to make sure we were not ambushed.

Naturally, progress was not that quick. Often the undergrowth was thick, and with a large pack on your back it was difficult to move fast under falling branches or bamboo.

We started at about 8.00 am, and a halt was usually called for tea at midday. We then opened our wireless and tuned into the Battalion net to report progress, etc. There was also an early morning and evening call after 6.30 am and 5.30 pm.

Patrolling then continued until about 3.30 pm, after which a proper halt was made and a base prepared for the night. If possible, this would be in a place that could easily be defended and was near a stream for water. Sentries were posted and small patrols sent out in every direction to make certain that the enemy were not in the immediate vicinity. (On these little patrols the large pack was left in the platoon or company base.)

Little *bashas* were made, each for two people. One poncho was laid on the ground and another strung up on a pole between two sticks to form a small tent. Each man had his own blanket. At night we changed into a warmer shirt, washed our feet, changed our socks and put gym shoes on. As it rained hard most days, this also gave us an opportunity to dry our clothes. You could hear the rain coming, the drops hitting the leaves on the jungle canopy as the storm approached, then after a while coming through and making you dripping wet. We didn't bother with our ponchos as they impeded movement, and in any event these tropical downpours made everything soaking wet.

We slept with our weapons close at hand, and one or two sentries remained on guard throughout the night, taking two-hour shifts. In the evening we had a cooked meal, a curry of lamb or goat meat, with rice and vegetables. Being mainly Hindus, Gurkhas do not eat pork or beef. In camp it was usual to have the water point on one side and use the other side to go to the loo.

October 1951

In October 1951 the Battalion was withdrawn from operations and went north to Sungai Patani to rest and retrain. Sungai Patani was also the Gurkha Recruit Training Depot. We lived in a large pleasant mess, and the men had good quarters.

We got back to peacetime soldiering: parades, rifle-shooting on the ranges and plenty of games, rest and recreation. We visited Penang nearby, and one weekend I went in a police launch to Langkawi, which in those days was just a small fishing village on the island but is now a holiday resort.

We were also entertained by the local planters, and most Sundays went shooting crocodiles on a nearby swampy lake which was infested with them. The mess was pretty formal, and we dressed up in mess kit in the evenings. This consisted of green trousers, wellington boots, white shirt, wing collar and bow tie and starched white mess jacket with miniature medals – rather different from jungle green!

November 1951

At the end of November we moved back to operations in South Johore, based at Muar (south of Malacca). I was now in temporary command of D Company, as Gil Hickey had returned from leave and was back with B Company. I was based in a horrid camp on a rubber estate at a place called Timiong Rinchang, about 25 miles from Muar. We took over from a Scottish regiment, who had left the camp in a filthy state, but we cleaned the place up. We lived in huts with tin roofs and spent a lot of time in swampy jungle which was full of long, sharp palm-like reeds with thorns on them. These were called *beltari*. Our days were spent wading in brackish water up to our knees, and finding a decent dry place to sleep became a problem. There were little hills, two or three feet above water level, throughout these swamps, but these were inhabited by wild boar plus their fleas and ticks. We often had to cut bamboo platforms to sleep on, but fleas, ticks, leeches and mosquitoes were our constant companions. We had one contact in this swamp when a couple of shots were exchanged, but the follow-up in knee-deep water was virtually impossible.

Our airdrops were larger than normal as our clothing demand was far greater than usual. The thorns of the *beltari* cut our clothes to ribbons – and were not kind to our arms and legs either! These were easily the worst conditions we had experienced anywhere in Malaya. Our feet suffered constantly from being wet all day, and the incidence of fungal foot rot increased dramatically. A patrol of seven or eight days was usual here – taking an airdrop on the fifth day out.

Chapter 3

February–July 1952

I was promoted to captain in 1952, and then another phase of our operations commenced. Not far away was the Labis Forest Reserve. This and the surrounding area were home to many communist terrorists, believed to be up to a hundred in number.

In February 1952, I was sent out with the whole of D company to try and locate them. We had information that they frequented some durian groves near the jungle edge. This became the longest patrol that I had been on to date; we were in the jungle for five weeks. I established a base in the deep jungle near where the durian groves were said to be and searched the area. We patrolled for the most part in platoon strength due to the numbers of the enemy.

I had an issue that was difficult to deal with during this patrol, when one of the riflemen went mad. He wouldn't stop talking in a loud voice, and none of us could make him stop. All commands in the jungle were given by signs or signals when we were on the move, and someone making a noise was a danger to us all. Even in camp at night we talked in low voices. After two or three days of this we couldn't stand it any longer, and I sent a patrol out of the jungle with him. The patrol met up with an escort from the battalion who took custody of him. We never saw him again, and he was discharged and sent back to Nepal.

We found many large old camps, but none appeared to have been occupied or used in the last two or three months. During this patrol my brother Geoffrey won the British Amateur Racquets Championship for the first time; I got the scores over the wireless. When we came out of the jungle, I discovered that King George VI had died and that we now had a new Queen.

What I had not realized (or had not been told at the time of entry to the jungle) was that this patrol was the preliminary to a large brigade-scale operation called Operation PERIANDER. The rest of the battalion took part in this, plus most of the 1st/2nd Gurkha Rifles. The area which we had searched was deemed to be free of enemy, and all the forces gathered around the eastern half of the jungle reserve – about 700 men in the forest and 300 or 400 outside, including patrols on the road by the local cavalry regiment.

March 1952

Gil Hickey had gone to Sungai Patani to command the Boys Company (recruits) at the Gurkha Depot, and Peter Winstanley had taken over B Company. He was an experienced pre-war regular officer, originally from the 5th Royal Gurkha Rifles. During the early phase of the Operation, B Company were fired on and almost immediately found a large, recently deserted camp, which had been occupied by seventy or eighty people an hour or so previously. They had split up into small groups and moved elsewhere.

Operation PERIANDER went on for nearly another month, but the enemy disappeared virtually without trace. This illustrates how difficult it was to seek out and kill them. With visibility down to 5 or 10 yards at the most, it was too easy for them to melt away into the jungle and re-form elsewhere.

April 1952

The Battalion moved north to the Kuala Kangsar area of Perak in April 1952. I was posted with D Company, of which I was in temporary command, and took over from 40 Commando. We were based in the Old Convent in Taiping. This was an old stone building with an attractive pillared courtyard, the former cloisters, in fact. The upper floor was unsafe and unused except for a small part at the front of

Robert's father (centre) with his dog Susan, 1/15th Punjab Regiment, Wana, 1931. (*Atkins family*)

Lieutenant Colonel Geoffrey Willoughby Atkins MC with his twin sons Robert (left) and Geoffrey. (*Atkins family*)

8th Gurkhas Boxing Team, 1945. (*Gurkha Museum*)

Officers of 2nd Battalion, 8th Gurkha Rifles outside their mess, Quetta, March 1946. (*Gurkha Museum*)

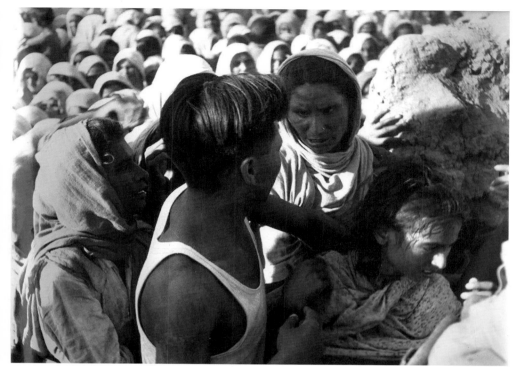

A Gurkha helping to unload supplies in a crowd of Indian women. (*Gurkha Museum*)

Rifleman Asar Sing Limbu guarding refugees on the dam at Balloki. (*Gurkha Museum*)

Refugees on buses.
(*Gurkha Museum*)

Temporary refugee camp,
probably at Bhai Pheru.
(*Gurkha Museum*)

Free air drop at Balloki.
(*Gurkha Museum*)

Refugees on the move.
(*Gurkha Museum*)

A Gurkha feeds the hungry.
(*Gurkha Museum*)

Horrors on the railway.
(*Gurkha Museum*)

Refugees crossing the Sutlej River into India. (*Gurkha Museum*)

Lord and Lady Mountbatten aboard an elephant, with Nehru behind them. (*Gurkha Museum*)

The officers of 1st Battalion, 6th Gurkhas, 1951. Lieutenant Robert Atkins standing second right. (*6th Gurkha Rifles Regimental Association*)

6th Gurkha Rifles soldiers prepare to deploy by RAF helicopters into the jungle during the Malayan Emergency. (*Gurkha Museum*)

A rare picture of Chin Peng, arriving for talks towards the end of the Emergency. (*Gurkha Museum*)

The impact of bombing the jungle – a two-edged weapon. (*Gurkha Museum*)

Cooking up at the end of the day. (*Gurkha Museum*)

Hazardous flying by the RAF into a cleared landing point. (*Gurkha Museum*)

A Dingo Scout car with Bren gunner up front. (*Gurkha Museum*)

Operating terrain –
the Malayan jungle.
(*Gurkha Museum*)

A Gurkha patrol.
(*Gurkha Museum*)

A Gurkha zeroes
his weapon.
(*Gurkha Museum*)

Gurkhas wait in a rubber estate during the Emergency. (*Gurkha Museum*)

The Sakai demonstrate their blowpipe skills. (*Gurkha Museum*)

General Sir Gerald Templer with Major Desmond Houston and a platoon of 6th Gurkha Rifles. (*Gurkha Museum*)

Gurkha 3″ mortar men during the Emergency. (*Gurkha Museum*)

Major Harkasing Rai MC*, IDSM, MM. A most gallant Gurkha Officer in Burma and Malaya, and fellow 6th Gurkhas Company Commander of Robert Atkins. (*6th Gurkha Rifles Regimental Association*)

A light-hearted 6th Gurkha Rifles Platoon about to set off to seek CTs in the jungle. Malaya, 1950s. (*6th Gurkha Rifles Regimental Association*)

Bha Ginta, notorious Sakai aboriginal leader, with Major O'Bree. (*6th Gurkha Rifles Regimental Association*)

Dead Communist terrorist displayed outside a Malayan Police Station as propaganda. (*6th Gurkha Rifles Regimental Association*)

Captain Manu Gurung MBE, MC. Robert's Second-in-Command in B Company. (*6th Gurkha Rifles Regimental Association*)

Robert with his parents, Geoffrey Willoughby Atkins (1883–1955) and Mary Ursula Marchand (1896–1996), Buckingham Palace, 14 March 1954, when he received his MC. (*Atkins family*)

Robert and Anabel's wedding at the Portuguese Mission Church, Singapore, 29 December 1956. (*Atkins family*)

General Sir Walter Walker KCB, CBE, DSO**. As a Lieutenant Colonel he had been Robert Atkins' 1/6 Gurkha Rifles Commanding Officer in Malaya and recommended Robert for his Military Cross. (*Gurkha Museum*)

A contingent of the 6th Gurkha Rifles march in the Victory Parade in Kuala Lumpur 1960 to mark the official end of the Emergency. (*Gurkha Museum*)

Anabel being presented with a ceremonial silver *kukri* on her and Robert's wedding day. (*Atkins family*)

Robert at his and Anabel's bungalow, Craig Robert, in the Cameron Highlands, 1957. He is showing off his new jungle boots to his new bride. (*Atkins family*)

Robert in the New Territories, Hong Kong, near the border with China. c. 1957. (*Atkins family*)

(L to R) Geoffrey Atkins, Robert's twin brother, for eighteen years World Racquets Champion, Anabel, Robert. (*Atkins family*)

Robert and Anabel with Corporal Suraj Limbu QOGLR (left) and Captain Kiran Pun MVO, RGR, who have presented Robert with a new *kukri*. Celestine (left) with her children William and Davina. Vicky (right) with James and Ella. (*Atkins family*)

Robert wearing his medals at the Gallipoli Centenary Commemorations, Westminster, April 2015. (*Atkins family*)

In the garden with Anabel. (*Atkins family*)

the building, where I had my quarters: a pleasant sitting room, dining room, bedroom and bathroom with shower; the best quarters I had anywhere. Taiping is reputed to be the second wettest place in the world, and it rained hard every afternoon starting at three o'clock; so regularly that you could almost set your watch by it.

Taiping was a pleasant town with a good club and a civil and military hospital and was the HQ for the local civil, police and military administration. The main north/south road and railway passed through the town. Battalion HQ was in Kuala Kangsar, which of course was the old capital of Perak and where the Sultan of Perak had his palaces. Naturally, I reported to Battalion headquarters, though as commander of the local operational unit in Taiping I had dealings with the District Officer and the Taiping police commander.

North and Upper Perak are very mountainous. There are two main ridges of limestone hills rising to 6,000ft or more, densely covered with primary jungle. The edges of the roads and the area close to the Perak River were mostly cultivated, with rubber plantations, oil palms, bananas, pineapples and maize.

There was one active terrorist unit north of Taiping, and shortly after arriving and settling in I went out with a patrol to get a feel for the area. We had a contact on our second day out, on a narrow track on the crest of a hill. There were signs of recent movement on this track, and I had gone up to investigate, when the leading scout was fired at. It so happened that Jitbahadur, my orderly, and I were close by. Poor Jitbahadur was hit in the right arm and elbow, and after an uncomfortable night he was airlifted out by a naval helicopter the next day. The pilot, Lieutenant Thompson, had been at Rugby with me.

Jitbahadur's wound, caused by a shotgun at close range, was unfortunately very serious. He lost his elbow and was invalided out without regaining the use of his right arm. We spent the next two or three days searching the area but lost the enemy, who were probably only two or three in number.

Shortly after we returned to base at Taiping, Angus MacDonald arrived back from long leave and resumed command of the company. I remained with him for the next few days and then went to Kuala Kangsar to take over Support Company.

Kuala Kangsar was a tented camp, except for the mess, which was in the Istana, a palace of one of the Sultan of Perak's wives. I slept in a tent, so it was considerably less comfortable than Taiping.

May 1952

On 30 May I went out on a screening operation, checking a Chinese village with the police special branch. The men surrounded the village to make sure that no one moved out through the wire, and the police set up a screen by the village gate which all the inhabitants used to go out to the estates to work.

Behind this screen, which was made of sacking, we had a recently surrendered SEP who had been in the area of this village. (We were in fact some miles out of Taiping on the Kuala Kangsar Road.) When the SEP saw a villager who may have been a member of the Min Yuen or a terrorist informer or supplier, he pointed him out to the special branch officer sitting with him behind the screen. These people were then stopped, siphoned off and interrogated by the police, without their knowing who had fingered them.

I was nearby with my Dingo scout car, a small armoured Daimler with a wireless in it, a 19 set which had a good range and reception, tuned in to the Battalion net. My driver/wireless operator called me and told me that 'D Company Sahib' (Angus Macdonald) had been killed. I listened in, and it transpired that Angus had gone out the previous day with two platoons and an SEP, recently surrendered, who led them to a small camp which he had attacked the previous evening. Angus had been shot by the enemy sentry and died of his wound shortly after. (This camp was not far from where we had had the contact when Jitbahadur was wounded and was probably part of the same unit). A rifleman was also wounded but survived.

June 1952

Angus was a Burma veteran and had been awarded a bar to his MC in 1949. He left a wife and two young children. As I knew D Company well, I rather hoped I would be appointed to command it. However, Jimmy Lys had just returned from long leave and was senior to me, so he took over.

Anyway, I returned to Kuala Kangsar and Support Company. A couple of days later, on 2 June, I was sent for urgently by the Commanding Officer. Peter Winstanley had been severely wounded and I was ordered to pack up and go and assume command of B Company immediately. I was also instructed to go with the RMO (regimental medical officer) to the 43rd mile of the Kuala Kangsar/Lenggong road to supervise the evacuation of Major Winstanley. We drove up to the 43rd milestone in an armoured convoy with an ambulance. The Lenggong Road was notoriously dangerous at this time. It wound and twisted through a valley with jungle and mountains on the west side and the River Perak to the east. These hills were the same as those to the north and east of Taiping and rose very steeply to 3,000ft or more within a mile of the road.

We arrived at the 43rd milestone, and shortly afterwards scouts appeared from No 4 Platoon. Soon the main party arrived carrying Peter Winstanley tied up in a sling-like stretcher made from poncho capes and two bamboo poles. He was in great pain. The journey down the very steep hill had been extremely difficult for the men carrying this makeshift stretcher. The doctor, Stewart Surman, attended to his patient and to a rifleman, Aganda Thapa, who had a wound, luckily not very serious, in his kneecap.

The rest of the company came out of the jungle led by the second-in-command, Captain (QGO) Manu Gurung. Once the lorries and armoured cars arrived, we moved to the company base at Lenggong, and Stewart Surman and his convoy returned to Kuala Kangsar.

Fortunately, I knew the Gurkha officers and most of the men in the company from my days in Rompin. Our base in Lenggong was right in the centre of the village, astride the main road. Company HQ, the office and my quarters were in the old schoolmaster's house, a small but pleasant wooden bungalow with a veranda overlooking a laterite basketball court, which doubled as a parade ground. The Gurkha officers' mess was in another wooden building, and the company lines were in tents on the other side of the road, together with the guardroom and *kote* [armoury].

Lenggong itself was completely wired in. Our camp, except for the road, was also protected by a high wire fence, and we put up barriers on the road at night. Lenggong was largely populated by Hakka Chinese and was the centre of a thriving tobacco-growing business. During the day, frames were set up to dry the tobacco leaves. There were also many small rubber estates in the vicinity.

There was no electricity during the day, but there was power by night to light up the town, including the perimeter. There was no telephone, and communication with the outside world was by wireless and the twice-weekly convoy which came with mail and supplies. This was escorted by a troop of armoured cars from the local cavalry Regiment, the 12th Royal Lancers.

The road continued up to Grik, which was the end of the line and the last outpost in Malaya; beyond this was jungle and then Siam (Thailand). Grik was the HQ of the District of Upper Perak, which was run by a British officer of the Malayan civil service (MS). A Company (of the Battalion) was based at Grik.

Once settled in at Lenggong, I heard a full account of what had happened when Peter Winstanley was wounded. Two days earlier, a recently surrendered SEP had given information of a terrorist camp near the 43rd milestone and said he could lead the way to it.

Peter Winstanley took the whole Company out, and Manu had commanded the cordon. Winstanley with No 4 Platoon attacked the camp, but a huge tree had fallen across the track, blocking the path. As Winstanley began to climb over this he was greeted by a burst of machine gun fire which hit him in the left arm and shoulder (he sustained six bullet wounds). Corporal Pimbahadur pulled him to safety, and the platoon spread out and charged the camp. The enemy fled after a short exchange of fire, during which Rifleman Aganda Thapa was slightly wounded in the knee. Unfortunately, the cordon was too far out from the camp, and the enemy escaped. This camp had been occupied by the local district committee member, Leong Chong, and his band of about thirty terrorists. Leong Chong had been a schoolmaster in Penang before the war and was now a senior figure in the 12th Regiment MRLA. He commanded the area between Lenggong and Grik.

A day or two later, we had a message on the wireless to say that we should be ready to move out on an operation immediately and that the commanding officer was coming up to brief me. Lieutenant Colonel Walker arrived later that morning together with another freshly surrendered SEP. A platoon of Support Company also arrived. The latest information was that Leong Chong had moved to another camp not far from the one which Winstanley had attacked. The SEP could lead us to this camp. More importantly, the commander of 12th Regiment MRLA, plus bodyguards, was arriving at Leong Chong's camp from the north for a conference in the next day or two.

This was a good opportunity. The SEP, who had only just surrendered, was a courier and was not due to return to Leong Chong's camp for a few days, so his absence would not be noticed. The colonel told me to give out the orders and said he would come as well. I briefed the Gurkha officers and we set out in our vehicles to the 43rd mile. The platoon from Support Company held the company base while we were away.

We moved up through the rubber plantation, then through *belukar*, tough overgrown scrub, before entering the jungle itself. I moved with the leading platoon just behind the leading section. Ahead was the SEP with Phang, our Chinese liaison officer. He was my interpreter, speaking two or three Chinese dialects as well as fluent Malay and English.

The going was very steep, with *attap* palm undergrowth and here and there large limestone outcrops, which were wet and slippery. We rested after an hour, then resumed our climb. As always, we moved in complete silence. Suddenly there was an odd noise ahead which sounded like the tapping of wood on bamboo, and I went forward to investigate.

The leading section commander, Corporal Aitasing Rai, whispered that the sound had appeared to be just ahead, and the leading scout had stopped. Nothing else was heard, and there were no apparent signs of recent movement. Lieutenant (QGO) Sherbahadur ('the brave tiger'), recently promoted from Sergeant Major, was the platoon commander and he suggested that to be on the safe side we should send out two small patrols to make sure we were not running into an ambush.

The rest of us waited while this was happening. I sent my runner back to tell the Commanding Officer what was happening. We then moved forward again after about half an hour and stopped on a crest near the camp which Winstanley had attacked a few days previously.

We were below the main ridge and not far from Leong Chong's new camp according to the SEP. We were now coming into the area of the commander of 12th Regiment MRLA's likely route; he would probably approach Leon Chong along the main ridge. I sent a small party towards the crest to protect us, with orders not to fire unless terrorists penetrated the area in which we were operating. Khagam Ghale was in charge of this party. He was one of the oldest and most experienced men in the company, although he was only a Lance Corporal. He had been on two frontier campaigns and had fought in Burma.

We went down the spur towards Leong Chong's new camp and began to spread out as we approached a dip in the ground with a stream in it. The SEP told us the camp was just ahead on the next little hill. Suddenly two shots rang out some distance from us, and there was a commotion on the hill in front. The next sound I heard was a long burst of machine gun fire: Sherbahadur was firing a Bren at the enemy camp. We all rushed forward and fifty yards on we came to the newly constructed and now empty camp. The enemy had fled. All their kit had been left, packs, clothes, food, papers, but there was not a soul in sight.

We consolidated on the camp and sent out patrols in every direction. Twenty or thirty people must have occupied the camp, and it appeared that most of them had fled to the south-west, away from the direction in which we had approached and towards the Lenggong Road and the rubber estates.

A few minutes later, there was a short burst of fire to the south, and shortly after this, Lance Corporal Ratnabahadur Rai arrived; he had just killed one terrorist on the stream to the south of the camp.

By now it was nearly time for us to settle down and feed ourselves. When all the patrols returned, sentries were posted. The men set up their tents, and Colonel Walker and I set up our quarters in the large, newly constructed and unused *attap* hut – which we presumed had been made for the commander of the 12th Regiment MRLA.

We had a problem with a huge *kadjura*, a large poisonous centipede about a foot and a half long with a body at least an inch thick, which decided to take up residence with us. My orderly tried to kill it with a *kukri*. He cut it in half, but both ends ran around as if nothing had happened. These were again cut in half and still ran around! Eventually, the creature was dispatched, but we were worried in case a living bit remained!

During the evening we carried out the usual wireless call and I conducted a post-mortem on the events of the day. We checked up on the sentries, and no one had fired the two shots that had alerted the camp we were about to attack. We wondered whether the party of Ko Lo Thien (Commander 12th Regiment) had heard any shots or knew that we were now occupying Leong Chong's new camp.

Colonel Walker told me to set up an ambush early the next morning on the entry route into the camp. I selected Lieutenant (QGO) Girmansing, commander of 5 Platoon, to lay the ambush. Next day, Girmansing and his platoon went out early, while 4 Platoon remained guarding the camp and 6 Platoon was held in reserve. We lay waiting quietly.

Shortly after 11.00 am we heard a grenade explode and bursts of fire from Girmansing's position. We waited, listening on the wireless for news. In a few minutes, Girmansing's signaller came on the net and said that seven terrorists had approached the ambush position, two had been killed and they were following blood trails from the wounded. I spoke with Girmansing and said 6 Platoon would come up to help and that Colonel Walker and I would also come up to see what had happened.

We were met by Girmansing when we arrived. The ambush had been set on the main ridge, where there was an animal track. A large tree had fallen here, creating a small clearing with sunlight filtering

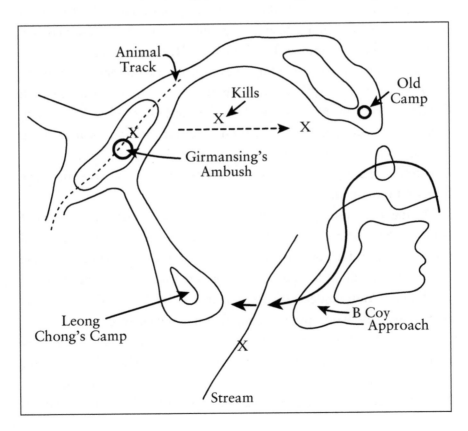

in. Lieutenant Girmansing had waited for the enemy party to enter the clearing and had rolled a grenade among them which triggered the ambush.

Soon after we arrived there was another burst of fire, and one of the section commanders returned, saying that two more terrorists had been accounted for. Even when badly wounded they had died bravely, defending themselves.

We set up our command post on the trunk of the large fallen tree and listened into the Battalion net, while Colonel Walker spoke with the Tactical Adjutant at Battalion HQ in Kuala Kangsar to report what was happening. A rather nice walking stick was found near our fallen tree, made from a bamboo root with the end carved, and the SEP who had come up with us told us that this had belonged to Ko Lo Thien. The four bodies so far recovered were those of his bodyguards, and the search was widening for the others. It was thought that all the enemy party must have been wounded, either by the grenade or by the initial bursts of fire. There were blood trails leading into the valley to the east of the spur which we were on. Girmansing and his men searched in that direction, while Lieutenant Narsuba Gurung with 6 Platoon searched to the north and west.

About an hour later, there was firing some way to the east, and Girmansing and his patrol returned some time after. They had accounted for two more of the enemy who had holed up in some rocks about 800 yards from the ambush position. This was not very far from the old camp that Major Winstanley had attacked.

The dead were roped to bamboo poles. One was the political Commissar of 12th Regiment MRLA, so an important figure, identified by the SEP. He had been badly wounded by the exploding grenade, the bolt of which was embedded in his thigh. That he had subsequently managed to run half a mile through steep and difficult country and then fight for his life when cornered shows how tough the human body is – and how determined an enemy we were fighting.

Unfortunately, however, Ko Lo Thien seemed to have eluded us so far.

We patrolled all around our camp and returned in the early evening, had our food and slept. Now that our cover was blown, the Colonel decided we should move back to Lenggong the following day.

The next morning, we had begun to pack up the camp after we had eaten and were nearly ready to move off, when the peace of the morning was shattered by a burst of machine gun fire just to the south. Lance Corporal Aitasing Rai sent a runner up from his post just outside the edge of the camp to say that a lone terrorist had been killed; presumably, a courier coming to Leong Chong's camp and unaware of recent events. This slightly delayed our departure as we had a look round the area in case of any fresh tracks.

We got on to the main road at the 43rd mile about midday, with the enemy dead on their poles. When we got to Lengong, the bodies were left outside the police station for the population to see – rather unpleasant, but necessary for us to make the locals realize that the bandits in the jungle were getting killed.

The Commanding Officer returned to Kuala Kangsar, and we cleaned ourselves up. Two days later, Radio Malaya came up to Lenggong with the convoy and recorded an interview with me about the operation. This was broadcast the next evening.

As soon as we had rested, the search for Leong Chong and his gang resumed. It was suspected that the villages near the 43rd milestone were supplying food and supplies to the terrorists in the jungle, and I sent 4 Platoon to operate in this area. Lieutenant Girmansing was later awarded an MC for his part in the operation. He later became second-in-command of B Company and was promoted to Captain (QGO) when Captain Manu Gurung went on leave. Manu became the Gurkha Major of the Depot at Sungai Patani.

On 10 June (or thereabouts) we had a visit from the General Officer Commanding Malaya Command, General Stockwell. He was interested in what was happening in Lenggong. A lot had occurred in a week!

A few days later, another SEP arrived with more information. He had just surrendered and said he knew where Leong Chong was now based.

He had moved up the road a bit and was apparently in an area near the 44th mile, so I took two platoons out early the next morning. We left camp about 3.30 am, and our trucks dumped us by the 43rd mile and drove further down the road before returning. We walked back down to the 44th mile and then entered the jungle. This part was extremely steep, with lots of gullies intersected by streams. As we made our way forward, the SEP kept saying the camp was over the next ridge, the next ridge, and so on. Eventually, our leading scouts, with the SEP and I nearby, were fired on. We returned fire with a Bren gun and charged. I had the feeling that the SEP knew exactly where the camp was but had failed to tell us properly because his old friends were there.

The camp was a mess. The terrorists had fled leaving everything except their weapons, food, clothes and a lot of papers. We spent another two days scouring the area but could not find a trail. They had split up into small groups and melted away. I went back to base with half the men and left the rest of 4 Platoon in the area to ambush the track leading into the camp.

During our charge into this camp, we had disturbed a wild boar's 'nest', a huge pile of sticks and leaves. The mother and most of her piglets ran off, but two little pigs were picked up by the men. They were adorable, covered with silky pale brown fur with two yellow stripes down their backs. Their little snouts were soft, and they were quite fearless. Corporal Aitasing put them both in his haversack and they came back to the camp with us. To begin with they were bottle-fed as they were very young. They became extremely tame and were highly intelligent. They answered to their names – Chanti and Branti – and came when called. They had the run of our camp and were great favourites with the men. As they got bigger they ate scraps from the cookhouse and grew fast.

Our hunt continued for Leong Chong and his gang of insurgents. North of Lenggong, one of his lieutenants, a man called Kwai Wah, was operating. We had information that he was meeting some Chinese tappers on a small rubber estate, and I took a platoon out to ambush him. We went out before dawn and were in position before the tappers came to work at about 6.30 am.

We lay in waiting in the undergrowth at the edge of the estate, watching the people working, moving from tree to tree to strip a bit of bark off with their tapping knives. Underneath this cut they placed a cup on a wire attached to the tree. Later they came back to collect in a large bucket the white latex that had run into the cup. When all their trees were cut, they returned home and we relaxed.

We camped in the jungle some way off the estate. Next morning, before the tappers arrived, a young wild boar was snuffling about looking for roots. Suddenly we saw movement on the edge of the rubber plantation, and out crept a tiger, low and cat-like, stalking the unsuspecting pig. The tiger got closer and then with a sudden dash and a leap landed on the boar's back. The pig bucked and screamed, and the tiger killed it with a bite to the neck. We had had a grandstand view, the kill taking place perhaps 20 or 30 yards from our position. The tiger then dragged the dead pig into the edge of the jungle and began to eat it, or so we presumed.

We didn't often see tigers, although we knew when they were about. We saw their paw marks and occasionally would hear them growl if we got close, often at night if we were moving in or out of the jungle. One day I came to a large fallen tree and as I stood on top of the trunk, there was a tiger was on the ground just below me. I froze, the tiger eyed me and then it stalked off, much to my relief! The Malayan tiger is smaller than its Indian cousin but is still a large and very formidable animal.

Kwai Wah and his gang didn't appear while we were in the ambush, so we went back to Lenggong after four days.

Shortly after this we had another contact with Leong Chong's party in the jungle in the area of the 42nd milestone. I was on a spur with Company HQ, and various small patrols were working out from our base. Jitaram (of Rompin fame) and his section exchanged fire with s small party of terrorists. There were no casualties on either side. Generally speaking, you only had about half a second in which to aim and fire before the enemy disappeared. You had to be very alert, with your weapon more or less at the ready, to get a successful shot.

We had a small firing range at each company base and fired our weapons as frequently as possible. This was usually done the day after we had come in from patrol. The first day was spent washing, cleaning and checking our weapons and kit – and resting.

On another patrol in the Lenggong area I had an unpleasant experience. I was lying in an ambush position on a small track leading into an old enemy camp next to my Bren gunner. Suddenly I felt something crawling on my leg. It moved and contracted. The Bren gunner whispered, 'Don't move! Snake.'

The snake moved across one leg, my buttocks and then up by my side and away into the undergrowth. It was nearly 5ft long, bright green and poisonous.

Snakes really didn't worry us much. The main problems in the jungle, apart from the undergrowth and bamboo (in bamboo jungle), were ants and leeches. Mosquitoes were also a nuisance, particularly bad in disused rubber estates; they bred in the water-filled latex cups. In the hilly area around Lenggong, once we were fairly high up, we were hardly troubled by leeches or mosquitoes. There were a lot of little wasps and some hornets in the jungle which gave painful stings. We all carried half a cut onion in our pouches, the juice of which, if applied quickly, counteracted the poison.

There were also deer of various sizes and monkeys in the jungle. Monkeys were generally high up in the trees and could be a nuisance, chattering above you and giving your position away. On the other hand, sometimes they helped us by giving warning of an approaching enemy. Birds and butterflies were scarce in the deep jungle but were plentiful outside, especially in and around the jungle edge. Of course, many lived high above in the jungle canopy, 150–200ft up where they got the sun. There were other nasty creepy-crawlies which we came across sometimes, scorpions, huge spiders and centipedes.

If we left our shoes or clothes on the ground, we checked these as a matter of habit before putting them on. In swampy areas near the sea one occasionally came across tree crabs. These could give you a fright if you touched a bony claw and felt it wriggle under your hand. In some parts of the forest, we came across rhino, but these were rare. There were also tortoises of various sizes. Some were huge and could move much faster than you might think. They could also be fairly bad-tempered.

We came across small brown bears sometimes, and also elephants, particularly in Upper Perak, in deep jungle near the river. It was wonderful to see a herd of perhaps fifty or more bathing. There was another large animal we saw rarely. This was the *seladang*, a gaur or bison with huge horns. These were usually found in the *lalang* [coarse grass] at the jungle edge and could be very dangerous.

Chapter 4

August 1952–March 1953

In early August another SEP surrendered in Grik, a small town at the northern end of the Lenggong road. A Company was in Grik at the time, and after a couple of days there, the police decided the SEP didn't have any worthwhile information and he was then sent down to Kuala Kangsar but stopped at Lenggong on the way down. I spoke with him through Phang, my Chinese liaison officer, and discovered that there was a small party of terrorists living north of Lenggong.

We went out immediately and attacked a small camp the next day, killing two of the enemy. He also gave us more information on Leong Chong and Kwai Wah which, although it was interesting, was of little operational importance to us at this time.

In August or September we had two tracker dogs attached the Company with British other rank handlers. One was a spaniel and the other a large black Alsatian. The idea was that these dogs would lead us to terrorists after we had had a contact or discovered a newly evacuated camp, but unfortunately they were of little use to us around Lenggong; the terrain was so steep and difficult that after half a day the dogs were completely worn out. The average daytime temperature was about 100°F, too, which didn't help the dogs. On one hazardous climb I finished the day taking turns to carry the huge black Alsatian across my shoulders. The British handlers were not up to our standard of fitness either – and were in any case not used to the jungle like we were. After about a month the dogs were sent back to work elsewhere.

On one of these patrols one of the British handlers kept complaining of stomach ache. We were about six days in and very high up when he started to feel sick. I consulted Stewart Surman (the RMO) on the wireless, and he thought the man might have appendicitis. I checked MacBurney's point (halfway between belly button and top of thigh bone) and sure enough, the patient was very tender in this region. His appendix was inflamed, and I asked if he could be flown out for surgery. No helicopters were immediately available – and as we were so high up it was doubtful if a helicopter could make it in and out anyway.

Stewart instructed me on how to remove the appendix using a razorblade as a scalpel, but suggested that with rest the patient might be better in the morning. He made a remarkable recovery!

September 1952

In September we were moved up to Grik, and A Company took over in Lenggong. Although Grik was the last outpost before Siam (Thailand) and the road ended there, there was a track of sorts that went on northwards. Grik was the HQ for the district of Upper Perak and had a British District Officer, a police officer, a nice Malay, and a small hospital run by an Indian doctor. There was also a small airstrip. As in Lenggong, there was no telephone link with the outside world, but there was electricity all day.

Our camp looked over the airstrip and had wonderful views over the Upper Perak valley and hills and jungle-clad mountains beyond. We lived in wooden houses thatched with *attap*. It was a comfortable camp.

Soon after we arrived, the local police commander had information for us, and I went out with a platoon and ambushed and killed two terrorists just outside Grik. Another platoon ambushed and killed one terrorist a few days later. We had a visit from the Deputy Director of Operations, General Sir Rob Lockhart, an old Indian Army man who was able to talk to the men which was much appreciated.

October 1952

Late in October, we as a Company moved to Sungai Patani for a month's rest and re-training. The depot was commanded by Colonel Phillip Townsend, brother of Group Captain Peter Townsend, who at that time had just broken up with Princess Margaret. I had not realized how well up the men were with world affairs and I had to field constant questions about the romance and what was happening!

November 1952

In November we returned to Kuala Kangsar after a pleasant rest in Sungai Patani. It was rather strange being under the Battalion's wing after all the independence that I had enjoyed recently. Our first operations were in the Bubu Forest Reserve south of Kuala Kangsar. We went out, again with an SEP, to locate a large group of terrorists who were operating in this area, which was very hilly with limestone outcrops.

The SEP led us straight to a camp. It had a cleared area on one slope and was perched on the top of a hill. I put a cordon round it, led by Girmansing, and went in with an assault group to flush the enemy out. I was in the lead with my Bren gunner, Gobasing, next to me. We crept through the latrines of the camp and spread out to attack, but the enemy had gone. It seemed that forty or fifty people had occupied the camp, and that it had been evacuated within the last two days. Tracks led south, and then the enemy had split up.

We spent the next days looking for them. It was very wet and there were low clouds and mist over the hills, so much so that we were unable to get an airdrop for three days – a very unusual occurrence. This meant that we had no food for two and a half days, and we got very hungry. However, we did find some jungle food: edible fungus, certain sorts of leaves and the larvae out of a huge bees' nest.

After our airdrop we pushed on southwards. We found a few small camps, fairly recently used, but no signs of the large party that had been in the camp the SEP led us to. When we got to the south of the forest reserve we received a final airdrop. This was in a large clearing, and as we waited for the aeroplane to arrive, two fully grown rhinos appeared, grazing in the centre of the clearing. I was worried they would be injured by the airdrop, so we started a fire. We would have had one anyway, to make smoke so that our position was visible from the air, but it was enough to move the rhinos off, and we didn't see them again.

December 1952

I only spent a month in Kuala Kangsar and then we moved back to Taiping to the Old Convent. In the early part of December we operated north of Taiping and went high up into the mountains. We spent two or three days above the jungle line and got cold at night. The peaks here were covered in scrub, on which moss grew in profusion. The views were spectacular, and we could see the Indian Ocean to the west beyond ridge after ridge of hills.

When we got back to base I had a pleasant surprise; it had been arranged for me to go on leave to Hong Kong for Christmas and return early in the New Year. I got the train to Singapore and boarded a troopship, which took three or four days to reach Hong Kong. I was fairly well off at the time, for with little chance to spend any money over the last year or so I had built up a healthy bank balance.

I met up with some old friends who had been with me in Quetta in 1946. They had just been in Korea; the war there was still active. They were in a gunner regiment and were very hospitable. I spent Christmas with them and New Year in the yacht club, returning on another troopship and getting back to Taiping feeling the better for the change of climate.

January 1953

Operations continued without much success. On one day in January or February there was an attempt to blow up the main north/south railway between Taiping and Kuala Kangsar, and I went down with the whole company to investigate as it was reported that there was a large body of terrorists involved.

We went down a track off the main road to the place where a bomb had been detonated. Various fish plates on the railway line had also been tampered with, but this had not stopped the train. We searched the area and, as was our usual drill, spread out as we crossed a defile. I sent a platoon up each side of this to clear it and moved down the centre with Company HQ and a platoon in reserve.

This was in a partly cultivated area with fairly good visibility but also with areas of scrub jungle on the higher ground. We found nothing and returned to base.

A few days later, an SEP surrendered in Kuala Kangsar, and it so happened that I was there on a conference with the Colonel and the other company commanders. I was about to return to Taiping but had a word with Cyril Keel, the police special branch officer in Kuala Kangsar, who was with the SEP. The SEP recognized me! Apparently, he had seen me when we were investigating the railway line a few days earlier. He had been the leader of that group. They had holed up in the scrub by the defile, he had had me in his sights (aiming at me) and he said that had they been seen I would have been shot! They didn't open fire as we were well deployed, and they would have been at a disadvantage.

The main thrust of operations was north of Kuala Kangsar near Lenggong, chasing Leong Chong's gang. Support Company was now under Harkasing Rai, a Gurkha commissioned officer originally from the 10th Gurkha Rifles, who was highly decorated with an MC, IDSM (Indian Distinguished Service Medal) and MM (Military Medal), all of which he had won in Burma. Anyway, Support Company were on the trail of Leong Chong, and Colonel Walker was also using a battery of 25-pounder guns to assist. Harkasing Rai was calling down the artillery fire to where he thought Leong Chong was – often only 400–500 yards ahead of his men on the follow-up.

We joined in the hunt with A Company for two or three weeks. Support Company had several contacts and killed some of the enemy, and the results of this chase had a great influence on our future operations for the rest of 1953.

Cyril Keel had discovered that Leong Chong's wife, who was also in the jungle, had become half crazy as a result of the hard living and the constant fear of attack. She and Leong Chong were not getting on. In fact, Leong Chong had a girlfriend whom he met from time to time, a young Chinese girl living in the resettlement village near the 43rd milestone. Leong Chong wrote to her, and some of his letters were intercepted by the police.

February 1953

Cyril Keel himself began to write to Leong Chong as a friend who understood his difficulties. These letters were left in a safe hiding place, which Keel had discovered, and collected either by one of Leong Chong's bodyguards or by himself. Eventually, Leong Chong replied, and over nearly two months a correspondence developed. This was in the early part of 1953.

In the end, Leong Chong agreed to meet Cyril Keel, providing he came alone and unarmed. One afternoon, Cyril went into the jungle alone to meet the terrorist leader, who appeared armed, with three bodyguards. They talked, and Leong Chong and the bodyguards surrendered. However, Cyril Keel had other ideas and told them to wait. He would enrol them as special branch police, pay money to their families or into their own new accounts and make sure that they were not attacked. In return, he expected operational intelligence, full cooperation and information on what was happening in the Lenggong area.

They met again a few days later, and the four men came out of the jungle briefly for a day to Kuala Kangsar and were officially enrolled as Malay special branch policeman. Leong Chong became a sergeant, and the others were all made ordinary police constables. They then returned to the jungle.

At the time I was unaware of these events as I was engaged on a most interesting operation in Kedah. I was still based in Taiping, but an SEP had surrendered with information about a large group of terrorists in the Kulim Forest Reserve. This area was being looked after, or was in the operational area of, the 5th Malay Regiment. However, they were not very efficient, and the District Military Commander, Colonel Guinea Graham, late 10th Gurkha Rifles, asked for a company of Gurkhas to be sent up to carry out the operation.

I flew up from Taiping to Kulim and met Colonel Graham and the special branch officer Alex Voetsky, who briefed me. Alex was the most fascinating man, a White Russian who had been brought up and educated in China, then married a Pole and worked in Germany and France in the late 1930s. He spoke several Chinese dialects absolutely fluently, also perfect Russian, Polish, German and French. He had served in the Indian Army during the war and so spoke Hindustani well, as well as Malay! And of course, English.

March 1953

The very recently surrendered SEP had come from a large camp on the edge of the Kulim forest. It was, he thought, occupied by seventy or eighty terrorists, including the chief of the whole of the northern region. He knew roughly where it was but couldn't take us there. On cross-questioning him we reached the conclusion that it was in an area of about three square kilometres on the southern edge of the forest reserve.

I flew back to Taiping, and we arranged transport to take us out that evening after dark and drop us off within about three miles of the suspect area. We had a difficult night's march which entailed a river crossing, very close to a police station and a resettlement village. The river was deep and about fifty or sixty yards wide, so we roped a line across. I swam over first with the rope and attached it to a tree on the far side. We had to keep our weapons dry as we crossed. Not all the men were good swimmers, and Girmansing and I spent about an hour in the water getting the whole company across, about 120 of us.

We were all soaking wet, and once we had emptied our boots we set off through a rubber estate on a compass bearing for the jungle. We stopped for a rest once we were undercover, had a cup of tea and then moved off to the area of the suspected enemy camp. We made a base about 1,000 yards inside the jungle and ate our morning meal of cold curry and rice which we had in our own mess tins. We camped on a small hill, took off our big packs, stacked them by platoon, each with a guard, and sent out a series of three- or four-man patrols in every direction on a compass bearing.

We started to patrol in late mid-morning, about 11 o'clock; by then our clothes had more or less dried off. About half of each platoon was out on patrol, and of course some of the remainder were on sentry duty or on guard. The patrols began to return after a couple of hours, and two had spotted signs of recent movement to the north-west of our position. About 3.00 pm the last patrol returned, commanded by Sergeant Manbahadur. He had found the camp, or anyway its rough location, and had seen two of the enemy sentries at fairly close quarters. The camp was about 1,000 yards away and more or less west of our position.

It was too late now to mount an attack. In any event, after Major McDonald's death in an evening attack we were discouraged from trying these, as we were unable to follow up once it was dark. We made camp and didn't cook, as I thought it would give our position away. I went out with Sergeant Manbahadur and saw one of the enemy sentries. We returned and made plans to attack early the next morning. Naturally, we were all very excited at the prospect.

We left a small party in camp, leaving our packs behind as before, and set off as soon as it was light, Manbahadur leading the way. He stopped short of the sentry position and with Girmansing began to skirt the enemy camp to throw a cordon around its far side.

I went in the opposite direction (south) with the assault group and waited as agreed until 8.00 am, before moving slowly forward up towards the spur on which we believed the enemy camp was located. We came to a slope from which much of the vegetation had been cleared – obviously to give a good field of fire against any attacker. I covered our advance with one of the Bren gun groups we had, and the rest of us spread out and moved up towards the enemy camp.

It was more or less exactly where we had expected it to be, but the birds had flown, obviously in great haste the previous evening. It was a formidable position with properly dug trenches, and by its size seemed to have been used by at least sixty or seventy people. Clearly, the enemy must have seen one of our patrols or our tracks and decided to leave. We were certain they had not seen the patrols that had spotted their sentries. They left many documents and a lot of clothing behind and had clearly decided to get out quickly.

It took the best part of an hour to get the cordon and the Company together again. I had sent a wireless message to our base to cook food for us and another to Battalion HQ to say that the enemy had gone – presumably to the north and into the interior of the forest reserve. We set up ambushes on the entrances to this camp and later that day moved our company base near it. We then began patrolling and following up the various tracks from the camp.

We had a contact with two or three terrorists, one of whom was killed during the exchange of fire. Two extra platoons from the 2nd Gurkha Rifles were moved into the north of the forest reserve and came under command. We remained in the area for another week, and the operation was then taken over by the 2nd/10th Gurkhas, Peter Myers (Bob Myer's brother and father of Sophie) commanding the operation.

Chapter 5

April–November 1953

No sooner than we had arrived back in Taiping and cleaned up than I was called to Kuala Kangsar, where the company commanders were all briefed on the Leong Chong situation. It was of course a top-secret matter at the time, and we were told not to discuss it at all except with those in the room. We continued our operations in the Taiping area, going out at the end of April to the south of Lenggong near Chrendrah dam on the far (west) side of the Perak River. The Chrendrah Lake was very beautiful, a wide expanse of water with mountains behind. At one point I wasn't certain where we were and climbed a tree over the Perak River to take some compass bearings on a couple of hills and fix our position. I was perched over the water on a big branch, and below was a crocodile looking up at me and obviously hoping I was going to fall in so that he could have a snack!

May 1953

Early in May, we had information from Leong Chong. A party of terrorists led by Kong Pak, the commander of all the Communist terrorists in Perak, was due to meet him in a week or so and then move across the Perak and go north to meet Ching Peng, stopping at a place called Swollen Leg Camp on their way northwards. (Ching Peng was the Commander of the MRLA. He had been on the Allied victory parade in London in 1945, when he was appointed an OBE, and he held the honorary rank of Lieutenant Colonel in the British Army!)

One of the SEP knew approximately where Swollen Leg Camp was. It had this name because many of the Communists during the war had used the camp as a hospital while suffering from beriberi, a vitamin-deficiency disease which makes the legs swell.

The Commanding Officer instructed me to take out a small recce patrol to locate the camp so we could surround and attack it when we got word from Leong Chong. That evening, I went up to Lenggong with an assault boat and stayed there until the early hours of the morning. D Company was stationed there under Jimmy Lys. We went west to the Perak River, six of us including the SEP, carrying the assault boat through the rubber to the river. It was a blow-up affair with two paddles, so not very heavy. We crossed the river, about half a mile wide, hid our boat and set off, all before dawn broke.

Here at the far side of the river it was pretty flat for a mile or so and had been cultivated in the past. This area had been used as a dropping zone for Force 136 during the war. Once we reached the jungle proper we rested and had our breakfast (cold curry and rice) and a cup of tea. Soon the SEP got his bearings, and we began to climb up into the hills. We camped that night within an hour or so's march of Swollen Leg Camp. I was on sentry duty from two till four that night. We moved off early the next morning and approached the camp from the south. It was on a little spur, and a track ran up to it from the south-east. This was the one on which the enemy party would come, and it in turn came down from a higher ridge, so that the camp could easily be bypassed.

There was one hut in the middle of the spur, and the sides were fairly steep. I had a walk around with bare feet so as to leave no tracks. Later, I walked to the other end of the spur so that I knew where it ended. To the east was a fairly fast-flowing stream. My orderly at that time, Rifleman Dilbahadur Gurung, came with me on the recce.

We were there for about 20 minutes in all and then beat a retreat back the way we had come. The men all came from 4 Platoon. I reported on the wireless at midday that we had found the camp, and we reached the Perak River late that evening, arriving back in Lenggong at about 9.00 pm. We ate and went to bed. The arrangements were pretty poor, and the mattress I slept on was infested with bedbugs – the others had a similar experience. Apparently, these mattresses had been left outside on the ground under the veranda. I did not feel very friendly towards Jimmy Lys the next morning!

We went back to Kuala Kangsar on the convoy and I was debriefed by Colonel Walker and Cyril Keel. I then returned to Taiping late that evening. For the next few days we rested and practised the assault on a small spur I found near Taiping which was not too unlike the one at Swollen Leg Camp. I had a nasty bout of influenza, or something like it, in late May (perhaps the bedbugs?), and our doctor, Stewart Surman, came over to see me and gave me something which seemed to clear it up. The Colonel also came over and saw our assault platoon (No 4 Platoon) carrying out a practice attack. We later discussed the operation and he asked me how many men we would need for a fail-safe cordon. I said I thought two rifle companies; i.e. six platoons or about 180–200 men.

On 18 May we had a message from Leong Chong that Kong Pak was due to arrive with him that day, and probably would be at Swollen Leg Camp on 22 or 23 May. The Commanding Officer decided we should take seven platoons, the whole of B Company and two platoons each from A and D Companies. He would come with me to be in at the kill.

I briefed the platoon commanders and we set out for Lenggong on 20 May. We crossed the Perak River early the following morning. This was a fair undertaking, and the third platoon of D Company were used as handlers for the assault boats, which were marshalled by Jimmy Lys.

As before, we were across the river by dawn, and once we were all over we moved quickly into the jungle. Over 200 men take longer to move than a small recce patrol, so we had to push hard to get to the night campsite that I had used before.

We moved off again early the next day after breakfast and a cup of tea, arriving at Swollen Leg Camp about 8.30 am. I left 4 Platoon in the assault position and then led the cordon round the camp. Colonel

Walker stayed with 4 Platoon HQ. The near side of the camp had the rest of B Company, at the far end were the two platoons of A Company and at the opposite side of the camp from the assault group were the two platoons of D Company.

I was back in position by about 9.30 am and placed Corporal Pimbahadur in a thicket on the lip of the ridge so that he could see the enemy arrive. He was in hiding with Rifleman Dilbahadur, who was Pimbahadur's number two on the Bren gun. Pimbahadur and I were in communication by means of a long vine, which he would tug when the enemy came. I chose Pimbahadur for this for two reasons. First, I thought he was the best section commander in 4 Platoon, and second, I wanted to get him a decoration, partly in recognition for his having pulled Peter Winstanley to safety under machine gun fire at Leong Chong's camp the previous year. He was later awarded the Distinguished Conduct Medal. Dilbahadur, who was with him, was mentioned in dispatches.

We waited. The silence was broken by a single shot to our northeast, in the area where A Company were positioned. This happened at about 11.00 am. Nothing further was heard, and we sincerely hoped that Kong Pak's party had not been frightened off. Just before midday, monkeys began to chatter in the trees to the east, the direction from which the enemy were due to come. A minute or two later, Pimbahadur tugged the vine. I tugged back, which was the signal to him to open fire when the enemy were all in the killing zone. The Bren gun fire shattered the peace of the morning, and we charged. The camp was perhaps 30 yards from our position. Pimbahadur stopped firing, and I saw two terrorists disappear over the hill down towards D Company's cordon position. I shouted for the men to stop. There were a few shots, and it was all over in perhaps a minute at the most. We captured two Bren guns and killed six enemy, including Kong Pak.

Colonel Walker was just behind us and was well pleased with the result. I opened our wireless link, and the cordon troops came in. We reported to Battalion HQ and said that we would come out to our RV by the river the following day.

After a further search of the area we moved down to a site by several streams and camped there. We left an ambush on the tracks leading into Swollen Leg Camp. That evening, Walter Walker and I discussed the operation. We also discovered that the single shot we had heard that morning before the enemy arrived had been the accidental discharge of a round by a rifleman in A Company. He was given a rocket!

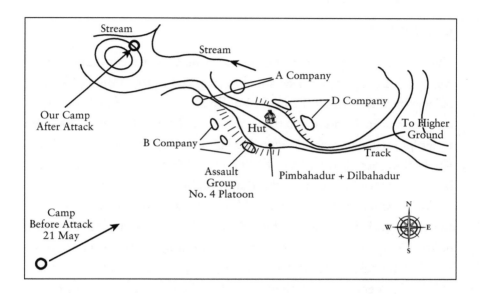

The following morning, we went back to the Perak River. I got stung twice on the face by hornets, which was uncomfortable and rather spoilt the day. We were met by Gil Hickey, who was now the second-in-command, crossed the river in boats and then got back to Kuala Kangsar and Taiping. The two platoons of A Company remained, ambushing the approach to the camp, and killed a lone terrorist a couple of days later.

Meanwhile, Cyril Keel had passed more messages back and forth to Leong Chong – still camped with his party near the 43rd mile but now left in peace. He had further information, and we agreed to meet him in the early afternoon on 31 May. I went with Colonel Walker, Cyril Keel and a small escort.

By the place we were to meet, a hut on the river side of the road not far from the 43rd mile, we found a message written in some soil in Chinese characters saying that he had had to leave.

We learned later that Kwai Wah had come down to see Leong Chong as he (Kwai Wah), following the killing of Kong Pak and company, thought that there might be a spy in the organization.

June 1953

The next big event in our calendar was the Queen's coronation. This was a holiday, and the officers had been asked to the Sultan of Perak's palace by the Crown Prince (the Rajah Mudah). The Sultan, of course, was in London for the coronation. I had just been promoted to temporary major, and Walter Walker asked me to bring his wife to Kuala Kangsar for the party. They had married earlier in Taiping, but he spent most of his time at the Battalion headquarters in KK.

We travelled in the Colonel's Humber staff car, picked him up at the mess and drove on to the palace, a huge building on the bank of the Perak River. We couldn't help laughing as we went upstairs. On the staircase were Malays dressed in splendid uniforms with *kris* (Malay daggers) stuck in their belts, but the picture was spoilt by the fact that they were smoking and had cigarettes in their hands behind their backs!

It was a wonderful party, held on the roof and with two bands in attendance, one from the 12th Lancers. All the notables in Perak were there. The food was excellent, and each table was provided with a large silver bucket filled with ice and four or five bottles of vintage champagne. (The Malays are basically Muslim!) At midnight there was a spectacular firework display, with the rockets and Catherine wheels all reflected in the waters of the Perak River, over half a mile wide at this point.

I cut my leg with a *kukri* one morning just after this party. It was very wet, and Aganda (shot in the knee the previous year) was tapping at some wood we were going to make a basketball post from. 'Come on', I said, or words to that effect, then took the *kukri* and gave the wood a swipe. Of course, it bounced off and hit my shin. The blood spurted and I clutched my leg in pain but managed to find the pressure point and the fountain of blood stopped. My reputation for first aid improved!

Aganda laughed and said it was no good hitting wet wood hard. I went to Taiping hospital and had three stitches without an injection or anything! It healed up very quickly.

Our next operation was in the hills and mountains between Taiping and Lenggong, where Leong Chong told us there was a gang of twenty or thirty terrorists (the same unit that killed Angus MacDonald). We didn't find them. However, we had one remarkable experience, when a young rifleman fell about 80ft down a steep cliff. I looked him over, and other than some bruises and grazes nothing appeared to be broken. He just could not walk or move his legs. This happened fairly early in the day, and at lunchtime I asked on the wireless for a helicopter to come and fly him out. There wasn't one available that day, but the arrangement was that one would come in and pick him up the following morning. We cut down some trees to make a DZ for the helicopter to land in.

I was with Lieutenant (QGO) Moti Gurung. As we could find nothing wrong with the rifleman, he suggested we asked the *yarbering* if he could do anything. A *yarbering* is a sort of witchdoctor, and we had one in the company. He only ate fish or chicken and did not drink. His name was Somanbahadur Gurung and I can remember his regimental number to this day – 2113 4323. He had been in Italy during the war with the 1st/5th Royal Gurkha Rifles.

Somanbahadur duly appeared and spent hours muttering over the injured man. It was a beautiful evening with a nearly full moon, and Moti and I sat up talking.

In the morning the man was perfectly all right! On the wireless call at about 6.30 am I was asked about the helicopter, and I replied,

'*Yarbering ayo, pujagarieko*' (the *yarbering* came and said prayers). 'We don't want the helicopter.'

I cannot imagine what the reaction would have been in a British battalion! But it was accepted by the signaller as an ordinary and natural event, which I suppose it was.

July 1953

When we got back to Taiping, I had instructions to go to Kuala Kangsar to meet Walter Walker and Cyril Keel. We were to meet Leong Chong. This time, we went up to the RV near the 43rd mile in an armoured car and an armoured lorry and picked him up at the roadside. It was in the early evening after dark.

He had one bodyguard with him, and they were both in uniform with their weapons. We drove to the house of Hamish Dongan, the chief of police in Kuala Kangsar; he was a Chief Superintendent and had a nice house. There were no servants about, and Leong Chong had a bath and was given a clean set of clothes, as was the bodyguard. We then sat down to a drink and supper. Leong Chong had a lot to tell us.

We discovered that Ko Lo Thien was now camped some way north of Swollen Leg Camp on a route that was used to go north up towards the Siamese (Thai) border, where Ching Peng was based. We were also told that it was possible that Chin Peng and Ko Lo Thien were going to be meeting in the next two or three weeks.

Couriers were coming on another route via Grik and south to Leong Chong in the next few days to give details. This party was ambushed, and six terrorists were killed by C Company operating from Grik. Documents retrieved gave an indication that Ching Peng would want Ko Lo Thien to go and see him – rather than the other way round.

To return to our supper party, we also learned more about Girmansing's ambush (June 1952), when Ko Lo Thien's walking stick was found, and discovered how Ko Lo Thien had escaped. He didn't run for it, but during the initial melee after the grenade burst he had hidden behind the large fallen tree trunk in the clearing then got under the trunk, hid himself under leaves and sticks and stayed there all day! We had used the tree trunk as our HQ for most of the day and had been sitting virtually on top of him. He must've had a terrifying day!

As I probably knew the Lenggong area better than anyone I got a rough description of where the camp was from Leong Chong. He had been there sometime in the past, and his bodyguard more recently.

There were apparently two Sakai *ladangs* nearby. The Sakai were Stone Age people, aborigines, who lived in parts of the jungle just as they had 20,000 years ago. They were rarely seen, they hunted with blowpipes and wore no clothes or shoes, just a thong around their private parts. A *ladang* was a clearing that the Sakai made to cultivate crops, mostly tapioca, with a fence round it to stop wild pigs from getting in. Neither of these *ladangs* had been used recently.

After the meeting, which went on until the early hours of the morning, I drove up to Lenggong and dropped Leong Chong and his bodyguard back near the 43rd mile, still in the dark. In the meantime, Colonel Walker was organizing air photographs of the suspect area which would become available shortly.

I flew over in an Auster to pick out the *ladangs*, which were clearly visible, and marked these on a map. Although the Company was based in Taiping, I spent a great deal of time in Kuala Kangsar and in Ipoh, where I saw the Protector of Aborigines. In fact, the day I was in Ipoh (the headquarters of the Government in Perak) Walter Walker rang me up and told me I had just been awarded the Military Cross for my part in the operations at Swollen Leg Camp. Pimbahadur got the DCM, partly in recognition of his bravery in pulling Peter Winstanley off the log when he was wounded a year earlier.

A specialist air photographic expert, a major in the Royal Engineers, came to Kuala Kangsar with the latest batch of aerial photographs. We could see the *ladangs* clearly and even the little bamboo fences around them to keep the wild boar at bay. He and I then made a model from the discussions that we had had with Leong Chong and his bodyguard, and we thought that we had more or less pinpointed Ko Lo Thien's camp. This was made easier by looking at a three-dimensional picture, which can be achieved by using pairs of photographs taken from different angles and viewed through a spectrograph. It helped that I had done a three-week course on photographic interpretation in Karachi in 1946.

In the next few days the operation to attack Ko Lo Thien's camp was planned, and Colonel Walker decided that, as the camp was a long way into the jungle, our initial approach should be made by helicopter and we would march the last two days in. This would mean that we would not have to have an airdrop, which would give our position away, before we attacked the camp. The helicopter landing zone would, it was hoped, be far enough away from the enemy camp not to alert them.

A, B, and C Companies were selected for the operation, plus Battalion Tac HQ. Walter Walker was a hands-on operational colonel and would be with us. Again, B Company was to play a prominent role, and I was to provide the reconnaissance and the assault party.

We all went up to Grik and spent the night there; a squadron of helicopters from the Royal Navy arrived on the airstrip the following morning. I went in the first of the helicopters, but the pilot was unable to use the landing zone as there was a tree in the middle of it. I was winched down a little over 100ft, and my orderly followed. Between us we got rid of the tree, a mere sapling compared with the surrounding ones. After a few minutes the rest of the companies began to fly in.

We posted sentries and once we were all present we moved off towards the Sakai *ladangs*, about a day's march away. I was in the lead with B Company. We got to the *ladangs* and camped on a hill nearby, a beautiful place, completely unspoiled primary jungle. I didn't sleep well. There was a bright moon which filtered through the trees, and the ground was covered in rotting leaves which glowed with a phosphorescent light.

The next day, we moved towards where we thought Ko Lo Thien's camp was. I went forward with a small fighting patrol to see if we could locate it, and we found signs of recent movement. A broken twig or a bent leaf on the path could be a clue. If a twig was freshly broken the leaves would be still alive, but they withered as time passed. You could tell if the trail was new, a day old or more.

I reported to Colonel Walker, then took the whole company with me, with 5 Platoon under CSM (Company Sergeant Major) Tejbahadur as the assault group. The other platoons spread out on each flank. We began our climb up the hill, then two shots were fired, and we charged.

The camp was empty when we got there; we been seen by the sentry. However, it was clear that Ko Lo Thien was not there. The camp was occupied, or had been, by just two or three terrorists. They had lit a small fire, still burning with the cooking pot over it when we got there. The rest of the camp was deserted and had obviously not been used for some days.

This was a great disappointment. We heard from Leong Chong at a later date that Ko Lo Thien had become suspicious of the aircraft flying over his position and had decided to move.

C Company was left in the area to ambush and patrol. The rest of us went back to the Sakai *ladangs* and were helicoptered out. As we flew fairly low over the Perak River towards Grik, I saw a herd of elephants bathing in the river. It was the best thing about the operation!

The Battalion was due to move to the Ipoh area shortly. I went out on one more successful ambush near Kuala Kangsar with 5 Platoon and Tejbahadur shortly before we left. We left just before dawn and were back before lunch, having killed two terrorists. They came exactly as we had been informed they would, down the track towards a rubber estate. One of them turned out to be a teenage girl. Both were very young.

When we moved, C Company was left at Lenggong and the rest of us were based at Ipoh in modern, properly built barracks, except for the Company detachments. I went to Sungai Siput, where the Emergency had started. We had been moved over to this area to mop up the remaining terrorists in the region, since Kuala Kangsar, except for Lenggong, was now more or less clear.

Our camp was in the middle of Sungai Siput, near the *padang* [playing field] and not far from the railway. However, it was completely self-contained. I lived in a pleasant wooden bungalow which also housed the company office and Ops Room. The town was surrounded by rubber estates, other cultivation and then jungle. I was anxious to avenge the death of a good friend of mine, Ian Christian, with whom I had served in the 8th Gurkha rifles in India. We had been in Baluchistan together and later in the Punjab Boundary Force during Partition. He and another young man had been assistant planters on Dovenby rubber estate, the largest one in the area, which had been surrounded and attacked by a large force of Communists in June 1948. The middle-aged planter and his two young assistants had been captured, beaten, tied up on the veranda of their large bungalow and then burned to death.

August 1953

Our first target in Sungai Siput was a large forest reserve just to the south of the town. There was a big Chinese logging enterprise in part of this, where the contractors went in to extract hardwood. This was done under licence and the operation was excluded from the total ban on any civilian entering the jungle. Although the Chinese loggers were checked and inspected, they were an obvious contact point for those inside the jungle to acquire supplies and information.

It was also rumoured that the local British doctor, who lived in a nice house overlooking the jungle where the logging took place, treated wounded and sick terrorists when the occasion arose, without reporting this to the police. He had a good practice, acting as doctor to most of the local rubber estates and driving unmolested around the countryside in a Rolls-Royce and a red Allard sports car. He also ran a clinic in Sungai Siput and did much good work amongst those who were unable to pay his fees.

I conducted a large operation in this forest reserve with B Company, D Company and a company of British infantry under command (1st

Battalion, Manchester Regiment). A large camp was discovered close to the doctor's house, but no enemy were located. The camp was within 200–300 yards of the edge of his garden and had clearly been used recently. It was also close to one of the logging tracks. (Geoff Hart was killed in this old camp while commanding C Company on operations in July 1955. He had been with the 2nd/5th Gurkha Rifles in Burma.)

On another occasion in this logging area, I was out on patrol when we found a disused camp. We made a base nearby and set up ambushes in and around the camp – and, of course, around our own position. I needed to relieve myself and went a little way outside the camp perimeter to have a pee against a huge fallen tree. I had my carbine slung over my shoulders. As I looked up I found myself staring straight into the eyes of a Chinese in a khaki cap and red star who was just on the other side of the tree. He had the very pale face of those who spend a long time in the jungle. He disappeared, so I shouted to the men and climbed over the log, but he had gone. We didn't find him.

To the south-east of Sungei Siput there were some bare hills covered with *lalang* (long coarse grass). The area, which had previously been cultivated and was now very overgrown, ran down to vegetable gardens on the edge of the town, where many local Chinese worked. We had information that some of these people were in contact with a small party of terrorists who came down fairly frequently to collect vegetables and even visited friends and relations in the town!

We laid an ambush in some undergrowth on the slope of the hill overlooking the vegetable gardens and three paths through the *lalang*. We went out early in the morning, walking in gym shoes to leave no tracks, and were in position before dawn. The workers came to tend to their vegetable gardens, and we watched and waited.

A couple of hours later, four terrorists appeared, dressed in ordinary clothes but carrying rifles. They came in by the path about 300 yards or so from our position, so we held our fire.

It was always a difficult decision to know when best to open fire, one that was left to the commander on the spot. I was worried that we would lose them as they mingled and talked to the people working on the vegetable patches. One of them left his weapon and went into the village.

We watched them for about three and half hours; they came closer to us on several occasions, but the fourth man had not returned. The villagers were also in the line of fire, so I did not spring the ambush. Our friend then returned, they moved off, and we opened fire at about 150 yards. In a flash, they dived into the *lalang* and the Chinese ran towards the village.

One terrorist escaped. The rest were killed, mostly by my Bren gunner in the initial burst of fire. We fanned out and searched the area, then went back to base with the three dead, whom we left, as usual, at the police station. Several of the Chinese vegetable growers were later arrested by special branch, but we didn't get any more information from them.

To the east of Sungei Siput, north of the main road to Ipoh, there was a large rubber estate owned by a middle-aged Old Etonian. Part of this estate was very overgrown with *belukar* [scrub], and terrorists were frequently reported in the locality, as they came in from the jungle, which stretched for miles from here up to the Siamese border.

Colonel Walker decided to mount a concentrated effort in this location, with three companies involved: A Company under Henry Hayward Surry, D Company under Jimmy Lys and B Company under my command.

D Company were the first to make contact and were themselves ambushed. I was in a banana grove on the jungle's edge at the time. The small arms fire came our way and we could hear the bullets whistling overhead. We ran towards the jungle edge and as we did so my runner kicked or struck an anthill – which, in fact, turned out to be a hornet's nest. The occupants whizzed out like fighter aircraft and several of the men were stung. Frankly, at the time, we were more concerned about the hornets than the small arms fire.

No terrorist came our way, and we heard later what had happened.

A platoon of D Company was moving along a track, well spread out, when the platoon commander saw a terrorist in the undergrowth about to fire. He fired first and charged, only to be halted by a *punji* (sharp stake) stuck in the ground. A firefight ensued, in which one rifleman was wounded and one terrorist killed (by the Gurkha officer). The enemy then withdrew. It was fortunate that the Gurkha officer had seen the man in the undergrowth, since most of the enemy were further forward and had prepared a defensive position around the track protected by dozens of *punji* stuck in the ground.

August/September 1953

A few days later, we were north-east of Sungei Siput on Point 1208, a hill on a ridge, when we came across a huge python eating a small deer; the legs were disappearing down the reptile's throat. It was the biggest snake I have ever seen. I paced the length of it, eight long paces, so it was 24 feet long, or more. The beautifully marked skin would have made dozens of shoes and bags and must have been worth a small fortune.

We watched the bulge of the deer pass down snake's body. However, A Company had had a contact and two terrorists were killed, so we moved up to assist them and left the python to digest its meal. We killed a man in khaki at the edge of the forest; he may have been a terrorist but he was unarmed.

Soon after we completed this operation, a young British officer, fresh out of Sandhurst, was posted to my company as company officer. His name was John Clee, and his father had been the Governor of Sind in the Indian Civil Service.

We had a visit from General Sir Gerald Templer, the High Commissioner of Malaya and the Director of Operations (the previous High Commissioner had been killed in an ambush at Frazers Hill in 1951). This was a good visit but also the occasion of an unpleasant meeting with the Old Etonian planter who owned the rubber estate already mentioned.

As the local military commander I attended the meeting. Colonel Walker, the district officer and the local chief of police were also there, and it had come to the police's attention that the planter had knowingly harboured terrorists on his estate – in those days a capital offence.

The planter had an extraordinary story to tell. In 1948 he had come back unannounced from leave in England and found in his dining room several armed and uniformed communist terrorists sitting at the table having a meeting. One of these was an illegitimate son of his, by his Chinese housekeeper. He was told that if he so much as breathed a word of this he would be killed. He did not doubt that they meant what they said – there were plenty of witnesses, and other planters in Sungei Siput had been killed – so he decided to keep quiet. He had spent the war as a Japanese prisoner but was now living in great comfort again, and he complied with their order. So it carried on, and his estate was used as a safe haven and a staging post for years. He knew what was happening but wasn't keen to be shot. His elderly butler was one of the terrorists!

November/October 1953

General Templer was tough but sympathetic. He gave the planter 48 hours to pack and leave the country, or face trial for a capital offence. He left.

Shortly after this, we moved our camp to a rubber estate outside Sungei Siput. It had been decided that we were too exposed right in the town; exposed, that is, to watchers who could see when we were in or when we were out of the camp.

We lived in tin huts and had a stream running along one side of the camp. There were a lot of chameleons in the rubber estate, and it was amusing to watch them changing colour.

The thrust of operations was moving ever northwards. C Company in Lenggong had some success, but in Sungei Siput we failed to make any more contacts, although we patrolled and ambushed relentlessly.

We had one unfortunate incident patrolling through some *lalang* at the edge of the jungle, when a rifleman and was attacked and gored by a *seladang*. The other leading scout fired and killed the beast, but the man died from his wounds, quickly, through loss of blood. His femoral artery had been severed.

On another occasion we were in a cordon position on the edge of a cultivated area as a stop for an ambush that D Company were setting. This was sprung without success, but we were caught in the crossfire and had an uncomfortable minute or two with shots coming overhead and very close at times.

Chapter 6

December 1953–December 1955

In December, Donald MacNaughtan came back from long leave and was due to take over B Company when I went on long leave. This took place just before Christmas, which I spent in Ipoh. I flew from Singapore in an old Britannia aircraft which went via Karachi, Bahrain and Cyprus, where it had engine trouble. We landed in Nicosia and I elected to stay in Cyprus for a few days, which I enjoyed.

January–May 1954

I was in England for most of 1954. The main event of my leave was going to Buckingham Palace on 14 March to an investiture where I received my MC from Queen Elizabeth the Queen Mother. My father and mother came, and we went out to lunch afterwards at the Junior Carlton Club, which I belonged to at the time.

In April Geoffrey came over from Chicago, and I watched the final of the World Racquets Championship at Queens Club in which he beat Jim Dear. I had an excellent seat in the front row.

Later that month, Geoffrey married Pippa Fulljames, and I was his best man. Afterwards, Henry Pownall and I went out with Jennifer Fulljames and Christina Smith, who were bridesmaids.

I spent the first three months of my leave mainly at Dippenhall, near Farnham, where my mother was living with her second husband, Geoffrey Marchand. I also spent some time in Devon, where my father was living, and of course in London, later taking over a room in the flat that Geoffrey had been in, in The Boltons.

May-November 1954

From the end of May until August I was on a company commander's course at the School of Infantry at Westminster. I shared a room there with Peter Myers, who was also on the course. I saw a lot of David Higham during my leave, and we went to Henley, Wimbledon and various parties together.

My mother's marriage to Geoffrey Marchand broke down during the late summer, partly due to the fact that she fed her pekes and not Geoffrey, but also because she discovered that he was sleeping with Louise, the cook-housekeeper. The split caused endless house-hunting problems, but eventually she found a cottage in Debach, near Ipswich. I took a lease on this for her. Later, my father moved into it as well. The last month of my leave was spent organizing the house and garden.

I returned to Malaya on a troopship. The voyage took a little over a month and I was in demand as a lecturer on board ship, talking about Malaya. As usual, we stopped on the way in Colombo, where I saw my cousin Kathy Atkinson (née Atkins).

November 1954

I arrived back with the Battalion at Ipoh at the beginning of November. With a new commanding officer, the atmosphere in the Battalion was very different. The new colonel was 'Speedy' Bredin, an officer from the Dorset Regiment.

All the companies had company commanders senior to me, except for Support Company under Harkasing Rai. For a short time, while MacNaughtan was on a short leave, I commanded B Company and was again based at Sungei Siput.

Just before Christmas, we had a visit from the GOC (General Officer Commanding) Malaya, and Colonel Bredin came out in the jungle with me. This was not in Sungei Siput but south of Ipoh in a flat bamboo forest near Tanjong Malim.

We marched for a day and camped as usual at night. The next day, a helicopter arrived and the GOC got out to visit us. Speedy Bredin started to get into the helicopter to go back with the General, but with an ADC and another staff officer, the helicopter was already overloaded. The pilot, who was from the Australian Air Force and had little respect for age and rank, said, 'Get out, bud, we are overloaded. You will have to walk'!

I remained in the jungle, and Colonel Bredin walked out with a section of mine, who later came back to join us. We were there over Christmas. On Christmas day when I got out of bed I had a shock. Underneath me was a squashed and dead snake, which I must have rolled on during the night; it had probably come in to my little tent to get water. I was lucky it didn't bite me!

The RAF were working and gave us a drop. We had a pleasant day as our camp was in a bamboo grove with a small river running through it in which we washed and bathed. The water wasn't very deep, a foot or so, but very clear and ran over gravel. The men caught a lot of small fish which they fried up – they tasted rather like whitebait.

December 1954

A lot of things had happened while I was on leave. On 1 January 1954 I was nominated man of the year by the *Straits Times*! This was the result of various successful operations in 1953, Army PR and the fact that the prosecution of the Emergency was still foremost in everyone's minds at the time.

Leong Chong was found out and suffered a terrible death at the hands of Kwai Wah, who had intercepted a note being sent out to Leong Chong's girlfriend at the village at the 43rd mile. She was tied to a rubber tree and had her throat cut. Kwai Wah then returned to Leong Chong's camp and murdered him, by tying a rope around his feet and a noose round his neck and then playing tug-of-war. Fortunately, Kwai Wah did not question Leong Chong, so the full extent of what we had learnt from him was never discovered. His bodyguards were not discovered and they immediately surrendered, telling the story to Cyril Keel. Jimmy Lys, with the patrol from D Company, collected the body. So ended Operation HUNTER, which was the codename for operations based on Leong Chong's information.

January 1955

In the New Year Donald MacNaughtan returned from leave, and I was again without a proper job in the Battalion. I became in charge of a detachment at Colonel Bredin's Tac HQ, which was now at Tanjong Malim, south of Ipoh by the road leading up to the Cameron Highlands. I acted as Tactical Adjutant and camp commandant.

A week or two later, I was put forward as a candidate for ADC to the Commander-in- Chief of the Far East Land Forces in Singapore. I flew down for an interview and a week later went down there to take up this appointment.

I was given a nice bedroom, dressing room and bathroom and lived with the Commander-in-Chief and his wife, Lady Loewen. The General was a 55-year-old gunner officer, a Canadian. He had been in the Norwegian campaign and in Italy, where he had commanded a division in battle. My duties were not very onerous. After breakfast the C-in-C's staff car arrived and we went to his office a couple of miles away, where I gave him a typed sheet of paper on which were his appointments for the day. I then went back to the house, Flagstaff House, and discussed Lady Loewen's day with her. She fixed the menu with the British Army cook and if she wanted a hair appointment or something, I organized that for her. I sometimes took the dog for a walk.

I had a small staff car for my own use. Sometimes I went to the office, especially if there was a visit to plan. The MA (military assistant) did the C-in-C's paperwork and liaised with the Chief of Staff, a Major General, who also had a staff officer to help him. There were also a few clerks and a Warrant Officer in charge of them. So I did very little military work, which I found rather annoying.

Two or three times a month we went off on visits to units. This was when I had something proper to do. Otherwise I was just a glorified butler in the house, but living on the right side of the baize door!

If we went to a Brigade HQ or to a regiment for an inspection, I made certain I knew how to get there, how long it would take and exactly who we were going to meet. If somebody had recently been promoted, got a medal or had done something notable, I found out about it and briefed the General on the way. I would then prompt him, and he would then approach the man and say, 'Well done, so and so, congratulations on your decoration. I was interested to hear about the operation at such and such a place.'

This went down well, of course, but had usually been planned by someone else! We had some interesting trips, including one to Burma, where we spent about three weeks. We met General Ne Win, the military dictator, and stayed with the British Ambassador. To my horror, I was asked to drive his car, an old Rolls-Royce, through Rangoon as there wasn't enough room for me, the C-in-C, the Ambassador and the wives plus the chauffeur. I managed it without a crash – the first and only time I have driven a Rolls!

We saw the battlefields, flew over the Ledo Road and visited Mandalay and various other places. General Loewen had been stationed in Mamyo in the 1930s, so we went to see his old house. We went shooting for tiger, but fortunately none appeared.

We also went up to Hong Kong in a Sunderland flying boat and stopped in Manila and Sarawak on the way back. On another occasion we went to Saigon (the Americans were now there) and then up to Cambodia, where we saw the lost city of Angkor Wat.

Everywhere we went we had an aeroplane provided for us by the RAF and travelled in considerable state. On another trip we went to Pahang to the Polo Week. The General was an excellent polo player (handicap five). It was interesting to see the Malay princes together; most of them were in hock to the Chinese.

February–July 1955

My social life in Singapore was centred on the Tanglin club, where there was a nice swimming pool and some tennis and squash courts, also a restaurant and dance floor. I remember seeing Anabel walking around the swimming pool soon after I arrived in Singapore, early in February. I was twenty-eight at the time and she was only seventeen, so I didn't take much notice of her at first. However, we started to go out a lot together in July. An old friend of mine, Ralph Eccles, was in Singapore working for Unilever. We had been at Rugby at the same time and also at Bangalore OTS (Officers Training School) together in 1945. Anabel and I went to a party he gave, and it all started then.

In July 1955 Geoff Hart was killed near Sungei Siput, and the Battalion asked me to go back to take over his company. I wanted to go but wasn't allowed to. Anabel and I went up to see Peter Myers and his wife Anne at their house in Johore Bahru. Peter gave very good parties. In October my father became very ill. For some years he had not been well; he had suffered from sprue [a disease of the small intestine], and I now suspect bowel cancer. There was an urgent call from the War Office for me to go back to England on compassionate leave. I was having dinner with Anabel when I got the news.

I flew back on a Comet, but he had died before I arrived at the house in Suffolk. He had cancer of the bladder. Geoffrey had also flown back from Chicago. I spent a month in England helping to sort out his and my mother's affairs. My father had a military funeral in Ipswich. My mother didn't wish to continue living in Debach, and I arranged to hand in the lease of French's Folly (the cottage), which had been much improved. I went back to Singapore in the middle of November and then to Ipoh to return to the Battalion, taking over D Company as Jimmy Lys had gone on leave.

Chapter 7

January 1956–March 1957

The Templer era was now over, and the character of the Emergency had much changed. The terrorists were retreating into the deep jungle, and in about half of Malaya their efforts were on the wane. Once again, a civil servant was in charge of the administration, although operations were, of course, run by the police and military.

We were now going deep into the jungle from Ipoh or a base that we had at Tana Rata in the Cameron Highlands. B Company was also based in the lower part of the Cameron Highlands at Ringlet.

Without information from Leong Chong, and with fewer terrorists surrendering, it was more difficult to make contact with the enemy. My first operations in 1956 were from Ipoh towards the Cameron Highlands. We believed there was a large gang of about 100 living around the Highlands. Tracks had been found and several old but large camps located. Support Company and C Company had had brief skirmishes with the enemy, and Sergeant Baktabahadur of C Company was killed in one of these.

The Battalion had been allocated a troop of medium artillery, and this was used to bombard likely places where the enemy might be, particularly in concert with ground operations when tracks or new camps had been seen. On one such occasion artillery was called down near me, much too close for my liking. Shells were landing near where we were camped, and we wondered if they would finish up on top of us!

In early February I went down to the Jungle Training School at Kota Tinggi for a conference/training session to discuss tactics, etc. I was able to see Anabel in Singapore on two or three nights while I was there. I had asked her to marry me in October 1955, but as yet she had not made up her mind. We wrote to each other frequently, and when I was out in the jungle some of her letters arrived by airdrop, which was a nice surprise.

In the deep jungle we came across the Sakai aborigines more and more. There were different groups of them. We came across the Senoi mostly, but in parts of Upper Perak and up towards Siam (Thailand) there were Negritos. The main points of contact were their huts and little encampments in the jungle. Their houses were made of bamboo, and the platforms on which they lived were well off the ground and reached by a bamboo ladder. The side walls upstairs were of slatted bamboo and the roof was *attap* thatch. A whole family would live together in one of these huts.

The men hunted, and you would sometimes see their traps and snares. They used blowpipes to kill and stun their prey, usually small birds, monkeys and other small animals.

Some of the jungle we were in was completely unmapped. There were white spaces on the map, sometimes with form lines roughly indicating hills etc., which had been taken off aerial photographs. This made estimating and finding one's exact position difficult, but the RAF usually found us for our airdrops.

April–May 1956

Anabel came up to Ipoh for a long weekend in April and stayed with Jimmy and Honor Lys. We went to the Ipoh club with Jimmy Vickers and also to the swimming club in Ipoh. We got engaged in May, and Anabel and her mother chose a Ceylonese aquamarine with a diamond setting as our engagement ring. It came from de Silva's in Singapore. Unfortunately, this ring, and all Anabel's jewellery, was stolen from Quince cottage in 1993.

In May and June I moved up to Tana Rata with the Company, so instead of walking up to the Cameron Highlands from Ipoh, we started off from there and patrolled out towards Pahang and Kelantan. The jungle here, when you got the main ridges, was often very beautiful. There were orchids and many other exotic plants. High up, the jungle was more stunted and you got views of ridge after ridge of jungle-clad mountains in the morning, with wisps of mist rising from the valleys below.

On one patrol we followed the line of the River Telom. This ran through a gorge where the waters had washed away the rock. Salt was exposed and there were clouds of blue swallow-tailed butterflies coming to lick it. Further down the river, we came across a well-known, or should I say notorious, Sakai chief called Bah Ginta. He was believed to have murdered a policeman called Noone, a member of Force 136 who had dropped from a Liberator during the war to rally resistance in the Cameron Highlands area. Noone was never seen or heard of again, but his weapons and equipment had been found with Bah Ginta in 1948 or '49.

Later we patrolled the Sungei Wi, where there was a magnificent crescent-shaped waterfall. This was 40ft or 50ft high and perhaps 100 yards wide. We had trouble getting an airdrop in this area since we were very high up and the weather was bad; we didn't get any food for two days.

The area had also been bombed. I was not keen on the idea of bombing areas in the deep jungle unless one was fairly certain that there was something there. It made a mess of the jungle (an area which had been bombed, with various broken trees and branches, was very difficult to get through; the jungle was hard enough anyway). It also killed or injured wildlife. I came across a giant tortoise badly injured, with a bomb fragment stuck in its back. I tried to remove it, but the tortoise snapped at me and scurried off. I often wonder if it survived.

I flew down to Singapore for a long weekend with Anabel. We danced at the *Seventh* Storey, a Chinese nightclub, and also at Prince's, *the* place in Singapore at the time. This was a good restaurant-cum-nightclub and was run by a former Gurkha officer called Bill Murray.

To save money, I got a flight back with the RAF in a bomber, and we carried out a bombing raid in the jungles of Pahang. It was an interesting experience seeing it from the air. They kindly dropped me off at Ipoh airport, a four-engine bomber not being a usual visitor there.

August–November 1956

In July or August Donald MacNaughtan went on leave, and once again I took over B Company. I then moved from Tana Rata to Ringlet, which was a small village at the south of the Cameron Highlands.

Before I went to Ringlet I had rather a nasty experience. North of Tana Rata there was a Chinese vegetable-growing area at a place called Tringkap. As at Sungei Siput, in the morning the residents went out and worked in the vegetable gardens on the edge of the jungle, and terrorists came down to collect food and talk to them.

We had information that some of these terrorists came to a place where there was a scarecrow. Among the British officers it appeared that I was the only one in the camp who knew the Gurkhali words for a scarecrow, so I was nominated as the ambush commander. We went out early in the morning and, as usual, walked to the ambush position in gym shoes. We got there at about dawn, and I selected a position overlooking the scarecrow, on a little cliff covered with scrub above the clearing. There was a small stream in front of it.

On every side there was cultivation, but we were very close to the jungle edge. There were eight of us hiding up in the scrub, and our Bren gun was covering the scarecrow. The Chinese workers arrived and began hoeing and tending their crops and drawing water from the stream. Then a man in black with a hat appeared, as if from nowhere; he hadn't come down the path from the village. He made a sign with his hat, taking it off and putting it on again. We concluded he was a Communist terrorist.

He now passed very close to our position, walking fast and beginning to get away, so I ordered the section commander and a couple of

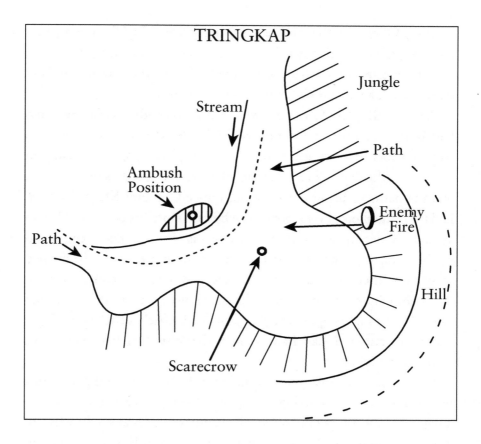

riflemen to grab him, since he appeared not to be armed. The men started down to get him, but the minute they moved, a Bren gun opened up on us from the jungle about 40 or 50 yards away across the clearing. Our Bren returned fire, and we charged towards the place where the firing was coming from. A tommy gun then opened up at close range, perhaps 15 or 20 yards away, as we ran forward. I could hear the bullets whistling past and could see them kicking up the dust. We reached the jungle edge, but the enemy retreated up the hill. Our Bren gun giving us covering fire had saved us. It had kept the enemy's heads down and luckily made their fire inaccurate.

We spent most of the rest of the day there, and I called up reinforcements on the wireless. We searched the area but found nothing. Of course, the minute the firing started, the Chinese workers had fled, and we didn't get the man in black. We heard later that the enemy reported that I had been killed. One of these terrorists later surrendered, a woman with a prolapse of the womb.

Back in Ringlet, Girmansing was now second-in-command and had been promoted to Captain (QGO). He told me about the two strange shots that we heard when attacking Leong Chong's camp in June 1952 (the day before his ambush). One of our scouts on sentry on one the paths securing our position, Lance Corporal Khagan Ghale, had fired the shots at two terrorists who came into his position. He had apparently not made a kill. Manu Gurung, the second-in-command of the company, had hushed the matter up as they were frightened of what Walter Walker would do! He had a tough reputation with the men, who nicknamed him 'the mosquito' because he was always around 'stinging' people for being slack or inefficient! Khagan Ghale had now retired. I had had no idea that this had happened until Girmansing told me.

There was quite a European element in Ringlet. Several people had retired there and were living in a group of small houses in the village. They were mostly people on small incomes who preferred to live in moderate comfort in Malaya rather than return to England, Scotland or elsewhere. One of these was Lieutenant Commander Dunbar, a VC from the First World War.

While in an ambush one day outside a field which was cultivated with blue agapanthus (for the flower shops in Singapore), waiting for terrorists to contact the workers, I saw a khaki-clad figure emerge from a bit of jungle. Suddenly I realized it was not a Chinese Communist but an elderly Englishman, or should I say Scotsman? It was Commander Dunbar VC! It would have terrible if he had been shot!

The Cameron Highlands were named after a surveyor called Cameron, who had been there in the late 1800s. The hills were up to 5,000–6,000ft high, and at Tana Rata there was a sort of plateau. The area had become a tourist resort and hill station, since it enjoyed an

English summer climate: warm days, cool nights and good for growing strawberries, roses and, of course, tea. There were several large tea estates and, in addition to Chinese and Malays, a fairly large Indian and Tamil population. Ringlet was at the southern end of the Cameron Highlands. The northern end was the Blue Valley Tea Estate and after that, jungle and several Sakai *ladangs* and settlements. We had one Sakai settlement near our camp in Ringlet.

Tana Rata had a golf course, a couple of small hotels, a hospital and two churches, as well as a small parade of shops. There were several nice houses dotted about. Gunong Brinchang was the highest mountain, and at the top was a wireless station guarded by a small contingent of Malay police. It was lit up at night, and the slopes used to be covered with moths which had been attracted by the lights. Some of these were huge and very exotic.

Julia, the wife of Bill James (then second-in-command of the Battalion), lived in a pleasant house in Tana Rata. She was rather nice but given to exaggeration. One day she rang, sounding desperate, and said, 'Come quickly Robert, I'm very frightened. An aeroplane has landed in a tree outside my bedroom window!' – or words to that effect.

I drove over in a Jeep, and sure enough, an Auster had crashed into a tree and was suspended close to her window! The wretched pilot, a young artillery officer, was up there too, injured but unable to move. The plane wobbled when he tried to get out of the cockpit. I got ladders, and after we managed to get him out safely, he went to the hospital to get stitched up.

October–December 1956

In October there were serious student riots in Singapore, and we were sent down to quell them. We drove down in a convoy and camped in various parts of the city, then patrolled some schools and searched them for arms. Nothing was found, and after a few days we returned to the Cameron Highlands. I managed to see Anabel a couple of times when I was in Singapore, and we planned to get married in December. I experienced some opposition to this from the Colonel, who wanted me to wait until April! Anyway, I got three weeks leave for marriage and a honeymoon and drove down to Singapore on 21 or 22 December with Jimmy Vickers, who was to be my best man. Jimmy's father had been Commissioner of Police in India and had been well known on the North-West Frontier before the war.

I stayed at Anabel's parents' house, and I think Jimmy stayed at the 1st/2nd Gurkha Rifles' Mess. One night, we were taken by Louis (Anabel's father) to a rock concert. Otherwise we went out in Singapore, had Christmas and swam at the Swimming Club and at the Tanglin. My last night as a bachelor I spent at Eileen Kilmartin's house and went to Prince's in the evening.

We got married at five in the evening at the Portuguese Mission Church.

The reception was held at the Burnetts' house, which was larger than Louis and Pilar's. Anabel and I got there to find that the caterers had only just arrived and nothing was ready! We therefore forewent our ablutions etc. and helped set everything out!

After the reception we went to Kallang and stayed at the Seaview Hotel, which was right on the seafront. The following morning, we gave a small cocktail party for the immediate family and friends. Then we went to the airport and flew up to Penang, where we spent our honeymoon at the Lone Pine Hotel. This was on the beach and was a lovely place. On New Year's night we went to a dance at the E and O, the Eastern and Oriental Hotel, with Colin Fisher and Carol, his new wife. They were married the week before us. She had been an airline stewardess.

January–February 1957

At the end of our ten days in Penang we drove to our house in Ringlet, a wooden bungalow with a nice veranda overlooking Ringlet and one of the tea estates beyond. It was about half a mile from the company base, on the jungle edge. We had a Gurkha guard on the house and two sentries at all times, so twelve men were in the area. My orderly cut the *lalang* back and made a sort of lawn. We also had lemons and an avocado tree. There was a tiger about, and we found pugmarks in the garden.

The house was fairly basic. We had no electricity as such but a generator which we put on at night. I went over to the company early every morning and came back for breakfast and lunch – and of course in the evening. It was rather lonely for Anabel, but she came over to the Gurkha officers' mess and had curry once or twice.

At the weekend we either had visitors or went out locally for drinks and Sunday lunch. We used to see a rather nice man called Bloxie, a retired Indian Cavalry officer who lived nearby. He had a pleasant bungalow and the most marvellous bower of bougainvillaea where we used to sit. We also had friends on the Boh Tea Estate.

I went out in the jungle once from Ringlet after we got married. Moti Gurung, a Gurkha lieutenant, was with another platoon at the time and had a contact in the valley below our camp. Anabel heard the shooting and didn't know whether I was involved or not.

We were only in Ringlet for three or four months, as the Battalion was due to go to Hong Kong. We handed over to the 2nd Battalion and all went up to Ipoh for a farewell parade and party, which was attended by the Sultan of Perak and various notables from the civil administration, the Army and the police.

Anabel and I went off to Singapore before the main body and had a week's leave there with Louis and Pilar. This was a pleasant break, and we visited all our old haunts, the Tanglin Club, the swimming club and various other places that we knew well in the city.

Chapter 8

April 1957–Summer 1958

We travelled up to Hong Kong on a troop ship and settled into peacetime soldiering in the New Territories. The Battalion was stationed near the Chinese border between Fanling and Shek Kong, and Anabel and I lived in the Shatin Heights Hotel. We had a pleasant room there, but it was some way from Kowloon or Hong Kong proper, or from the Battalion.

I had been to Hong Kong before and so had Anabel. In 1954 she had come up with Admiral Sir Charles and Lady Lambe, friends of her parents, in great style in the Admiral's barge. On arrival in Hong Kong, Lady Lambe was ill, so Anabel, still a teenager, had acted as hostess!

Before moving to the rest of our time in Hong Kong there a couple of incidents in Malaya that I've remembered and feel I ought to record.

A rifleman called Aganda Thapa (he had been wounded in the knee in June 1952) had one of his ears ripped off. It just hung by the merest thread of skin at the lobe end. I attended to it. The wound was fresh and clean, so I put a little penicillin powder on it and stuck it back on with a plaster. It healed beautifully, and Aganda was eternally grateful!

We had a pet deer at Ringlet, a large stag about the size of a cow. It was very tame until it came into rut. This was shortly after Anabel and I took over our house (Malay $200 dollars per month, or about £28!). It often came across from camp to graze on our lawn – the *lalang* had been cut around the house. One evening, I walked up the path to the bungalow (Craig Robert) and the stag would not let me pass. It put its head down and pushed and butted me. In the end one of the sentries came and rescued the deer! A week or two later, the poor animal was hit on the road by a water truck and had to be killed as the legs were broken.

Summer 1957

In Hong Kong, we lived in the Shatin Heights hotel for about three months. Luckily, the Fishers were there as well, so Anabel had some company during the day. The first parade was at 7.00 am, so we had an early start every day. At the weekends we went into Kowloon to shop or go to the cinema. Otherwise, I didn't get back till late evening.

Compared with Malaya, military life was rather boring. Occasionally we went to the hill called Sha Tau Kok overlooking China and watched the Chinese on the other side of the border, or rounded up illegal entrants. Otherwise it was parades – drill and a bit of shooting on the range. Of course, here we were limited in the number of rounds we could fire.

One week I was in charge of the guard on the Governor and the Army Commander in Hong Kong. I was stationed in the barracks at the bottom of the Peak, not far from the Government House. My father had been stationed there in 1911!

We had a typhoon in June or July, and the road to Shatin was nearly washed away. Shortly afterwards, we rented a place near the Battalion lines, a Chinese house in a vegetable garden. Anabel was very sick there; she was pregnant, and the smell of the vegetables was unpleasant to her. She was also very lonely as she was on her own during the day. There was no telephone, and our water came from a well.

We spent nearly two months there and then moved to a house on the sea overlooking the bay towards Macau. This was much nicer – but was very, very hot. We had to sleep outside on the veranda. My company was stationed nearby for a period of rest and recreation. (The companies took this in turns.) This was fairly good fun. We all swam a lot, played basketball, volleyball and football and generally didn't do much. Anabel had a yen for curry (as women get fixes on certain foods when pregnant). So, we frequently ate in the evenings with the Gurkha officers in their mess.

At last, we were given a quarter in Shek Kong village, on the military road running through the New Territories. It was nice enough but was next to a small car park and turning circle which was a bit of a nuisance. The best part of it was that we inherited the most wonderful amah called Ah Chan. She was a really good cook and cleaned like a dream, so we lived in the lap of luxury. The Fishers lived nearby, and we continued to see a lot of Carol. We spent Christmas with Gil Hickey and his wife Helen, who also lived very close to us. Anabel was now getting pretty large with the baby inside. This was the third Christmas she and I had had together. The first was in 1955, when she came up to Ipoh for three or four days. I remember we went to the club and she wore a mauve dress in which she looked very good.

February 1958

Early in February, Anabel had a show and pains and we went to the BMH (British Military Hospital) in Victoria, Hong Kong in an ambulance – the only time I have felt carsick! We crossed over from Kowloon to Hong Kong on the ferry; there was no tunnel in those days. Nothing more happened that day but the following evening, Anabel had slight labour pains which got worse while I was visiting her. I had booked into the Miramar Hotel in Kowloon.

The next morning, I telephoned and was told that Anabel had given birth to Celestine earlier that day (at 4.30 am to be exact). I wasn't allowed into the hospital until 10.30 am, when I saw Anabel and then had a look at Celestine. In those days, fathers weren't there at the birth – and in fact, I didn't even touch Celestine for some days, just looked at her with the midwife, a Sister McAllister, through a window. She looked very pink and rather red in the face!

Anabel was in hospital for ten days. She returned with Celestine to Shek Kong and got into the routine of feeding, changing nappies, etc. I could never do the latter – I did try once but was sick! We went on leave in April. As Pilar and Louis hadn't seen Celestine, we decided to stop with them for a bit before carrying on to England. We had a party at their house in Thomson Road after Celestine was baptized. Father Texeira, the Portuguese priest who married us, did the honours.

Louis's partner in Singapore wanted Louis to go over to Borneo to open an office there, so Anabel and I decided we would go with them and help set up the new office – and see Borneo as well. In the meantime, the Malayan Emergency had been declared at an end – so the main interest of being on active operations was closed, at least for the foreseeable future.

We all travelled on a local ship, which was comfortable in first class but not for those on deck or in steerage. We had a problem at Singapore as King, the bull mastiff, would not walk up the gangway, a fairly steep ladder all the way up the side of the ship. In the end I carried him up, much to the amusement of the assorted Chinese and Malay onlookers. King, who was very gentle, and Tina the Dachshund had to live on deck, but we visited and walked them frequently. Celestine used to pull King's tongue!

We went via Kuching and Miri and got off at Labuan. We drove out to the new house, which was close to the beach and out of town. It was a wooden house on stilts, with just enough room for us all. There was a wonderful beach about 300 or 400 yards away where we spent a lot of time. The beach looked over Kimanis Bay towards the mainland, and in the early morning it was possible to see Mount Kinabalu in the distance. Kota Kinabalu was still called Jesselton in those days! There was a little stream running on to the beach, with oil in the water! There were baby turtles and baby swordfish in the sea inside the reef.

Pilar and I collected wild orchids and made the veranda of the bungalow a veritable 'Kew Gardens'. There was a small Malay *kampong* (village) nearby, and a Malay girl came to help look after Celestine. She had children of her own, and one of them, a small boy, was killed by a python – but the father killed the snake before it could eat the child.

All through Anabel's pregnancy she had been complaining of pains in the stomach, but none of the doctors we saw found anything wrong. One early morning at breakfast, Anabel complained again and said she couldn't stand the pain any longer. I was in the shower at the time, and she went off on her own, caught the dustcart and went to the hospital fairly nearby. I followed and was met by the doctor, Paddy O'Neil, who said that Anabel had acute appendicitis and needed to be operated on immediately. Normally she would have been flown out to Miri as Paddy had nobody to assist or give the anaesthetic, but he said he could not risk the three-hour delay.

Fortunately, he was an experienced surgeon, having spent most of the war operating from the back of a truck in Burma. I signed the consent forms; Anabel was still a minor and I was her next of kin. She was then wheeled off to the operating theatre, a corrugated iron hut, and was given a spinal injection. This took a long time, and standing outside I heard it all going on.

Eventually, there was silence and I began to be afraid that Anabel had died. Then Paddy came out about 45 minutes later and said Anabel was okay and that her appendix had burst as he was removing it. Anyway, she was all right, but it been a most unpleasant experience for her.

She had a nice room in the hospital, and I became the night nurse and slept in a wicker armchair in her room – Pilar looking after Celestine. When the time came for her to have her stitches out, the nurse who was going to do it couldn't see! I had to help. We were both very impressed by Paddy O'Neil. He went round the whole hospital early every morning and last thing at night to see all his patients. He operated every day and had a very varied selection of illnesses to deal with.

Anabel returned to the house after eight or nine days, and Paddy prescribed 'ayer hijow' (green water), but in this case Crème de Menthe, as a pick-me-up! It took nearly a month for her to get back on her feet. The swimming and the lovely beach helped.

Late summer 1958

The Sultan of Brunei had built a huge marble, gold-topped mosque, and we went across in a launch to attend the opening. We sat in the second row just behind all the Sultans and Rajahs who had come to witness the event, and after the ceremony we saw inside. The trip upriver was interesting. We saw crocodiles and lots of proboscis monkeys in the trees at the riverside.

I now resigned from the Army, and we left Borneo in October and went to Singapore to wait for a boat to take us back to England. We stayed a few days with some friends, the Pursers, in their lovely house on the outskirts of the city.

We sailed up the coast from Singapore to Penang – not the usual way, for normally a ship would head straight to Colombo. We saw the hills covered with jungle, where I had spent so much of my time, fade into the distance as we sailed away from Malaya.

Appendix

Robert Atkins' MC Citation

74

FRONT   TOP SECRET.   Army Form W 3121 (Revised)

RECOMMENDATIONS FOR HONOURS OR AWARDS
INSTRUCTIONS

DO NOT WRITE IN THIS MARGIN

1. To be completed in accordance with current instructions and forwarded to U.S. of S., War Office, S.W. 1 in triplicate.
2. NOT to be used in connection with campaign stars or medals.
3. No abbreviations, except those officially authorized, will be used.
4. Whenever possible typescript should be used.
5. This recommendation will NOT be considered unless the personal particulars of the individual are correctly completed.
6. Only the original need be signed.
7. This form will be used for Women's Services.

If a casualty complete below :—   (For War Office use only)

Killed in action on_____   Citation No._____

Died of wounds on_____   File(s) 68/ORDERS/2196/1

Missing on_____   L.G. No. and date 21.7.53

Prisoner of War on_____   Previous awards_____

Christian or Fore Name(s)	Surname (in BLOCK capitals)
ROBERT EVERETT WILLIAM	ATKINS

Personal/Army number	Sub. (W/S) Rank	Present rank (Temp. or Acting, if different from Sub. or W/S Rank)
370460	Lieutenant	Captain

Unit	Parent Regiment or Corps
1/6 GURKHA RIFLES	6 GURKHA RIFLES

Honour or Award for which recommended	Award for which finally approved by War Office (For War Office use only)
MC	MC

Name (in BLOCKS) and official designation of initiating officer
Lt Col W.C.WALKER, DSO,OBE, COMD 1/6 GR

Date 27 May 53   Signature _____

Remarks of Brigade (or equivalent) Commander	Remarks of Divisional (or equivalent) Commander
Recommended M.C. C. deSaig Morris Comd 48 Gurkha Inf Bde Date 28 May 1953 Place Ipoh. Malaya.	Signature _____ Date _____ Place _____

Remarks of Corps (or equivalent) Commander	Remarks of Army (or equivalent) Commander
Very strongly recommended for MC Stockwell LIEUTENANT-GENERAL, GENERAL OFFICER COMMANDING, MALAYA (H.C. STOCKWELL) Signature _____ Date 8 JUN 53 Place KUALA LUMPUR	Signature _____ Date _____ Place _____

Remarks of Commander-in-Chief

Strongly recommended

Signature _____ Official Designation C-in-C FAR EAST Land Forces
Date 12 Jun 53   Place SINGAPORE

TOP SECRET

BACK   TOP SECRET   Army Form W 3121 (Revised)

CITATION

(To be completed by Initiating Officer)

DO NOT
WRITE IN
THIS
MARGIN

A. Recommended in respect of :—

　(i) New Year ~~~~ ~~ ~~ ~~

　(ii) Birthday ~ g ~ ~ ~ r

　(iii) Immediate Award (operational)

　(iv) Operational Award (other than immediate)

　(v) Non-operational Gallantry Award

＞ Delete descriptions not applicable.

B. Action or service for which commended :—

　(i) Place   SUNGEI CHEPAR, LENGGONG, PERAK, MALAYA.

　(ii) Date of action or period covered by the citation   22 May 53

　(iii) How employed   Company Commander

　(iv) Other detail :—

On 22 May 1953, in the LENGGONG area of PERAK, MALAYA, 370460
Captain R.E.W. ATKINS, 1/6 GURKHA RIFLES, was the commander of a
specially selected assault platoon which had been allotted the task
of attacking a Communist terrorist camp, where an important enemy
party of six Communist terrorists was expected to arrive on either
the evening of 22 May or the morning of 23 May 53.

The enemy party arrived several hours earlier than expected
on 22 May 53, but this officer had been in position since the day
before and was ready to launch an immediate attack at any time
during the day or night, immediately the last of the six enemy had
entered the camp.

Captain ATKINS led the assault against the enemy with such
dash, boldness and aggressive determination, in the face of heavy
automatic fire at only twenty-five yards range, that the camp was
over-run and captured in less than five minutes, all six enemy were
killed, and all their arms, ammunition, packs and documents were
captured intact, without any casualties being suffered by his own
troops.

The enemy dead included the most arrogant, ruthless and
important Communist political and military leader operating in
Upper Perak, who directed all terrorist military operations in that
area. Killed with him was his personal bodyguard, also a section
leader and three other combatants. The weapons and ammunition
captured included two Bren Light Machine Guns, one Carbine, two
Rifles, one Luger Pistol, three primed grenades and three hundred
and eleven rounds of ammunition. In addition, many important
documents were recovered, including written instructions from the
Commander of the 12th Regiment MRLA.

Ten days before this action took place, Captain ATKINS,
accompanied by three selected Gurkhas, had discovered this enemy
camp after a five days search in deep jungle. In bare feet he
entered the camp, made a detailed reconnaissance, pin-pointed each
sentry post and returned with a suggested plan of attack, together
with a marked map showing the enemy's most likely escape routes.
Later he guided the Battalion by night to an Assembly Area within
striking distance of the camp from which all troops were deployed
in such a manner that, even had the attack failed, the enemy could
not have escaped owing to the density of troops on the ground
surrounding the camp in ambush positions.

From start to finish, the fieldcraft, the guile and cunning,
the tactical skill and the aggressive leadership and personal
gallantry displayed by this officer were of the highest order and
worthy of high commendation.